Coaching Youth Football

FOURTH EDITION

American Sport Education Program

Official Handbook of USA Football

HUMAN KINETICS

Library of Congress Cataloging-in-Publication Data

Coaching youth football / American Sport Education Program.-- 4th ed.
   p. cm.
 ISBN 0-7360-6011-1 (soft cover)
 1. Youth league football--Coaching. I. American Sport Education Program.
 GV956.6.R66 2005
 796.332'07'7--dc22

                              2005005387

 ISBN: 0-7360-6011-1

The Web addresses cited in this text were current as of April 2005, unless otherwise noted.

Acquisitions Editor: Amy Tocco; **Project Writer:** Tom Bass; **Developmental Editor:** Laura Floch; **Assistant Editor:** Mandy Maiden; **Copyeditor:** Annette Pierce; **Proofreader:** Coree Clark; **Permission Manager:** Carly Breeding; **Graphic Designer:** Nancy Rasmus; **Graphic Artist:** Tara Welsch; **Photo Manager:** Dan Wendt; **Cover Designer:** Keith Blomberg; **Photographer (cover):** John Aronson; **Photographer (interior):** Dan Wendt. Photos on pages 1, 9, 19, 33, 49, 61, 103, 125, 141, and 155 © Human Kinetics; **Art Manager:** Kareema McLendon; **Illustrators:** Kareema McLendon (illustrations) and Human Kinetics; **Printer:** United Graphics

We thank Westview High School in San Diego, California, for assistance in providing the location for the photo shoot for this book.

Copies of this book are available at special discounts for bulk purchase for sales promotions, premiums, fundraising, or educational use. Special editions or book excerpts can also be created to specifications. For details, contact the Special Sales Manager at Human Kinetics.

Printed in the United States of America   10   9   8   7   6   5   4   3   2   1

Human Kinetics
Web site: www.HumanKinetics.com

United States: Human Kinetics
P.O. Box 5076
Champaign, IL 61825-5076
800-747-4457
e-mail: humank@hkusa.com

Canada: Human Kinetics
475 Devonshire Road Unit 100
Windsor, ON N8Y 2L5
800-465-7301 (in Canada only)
e-mail: orders@hkcanada.com

Europe: Human Kinetics
107 Bradford Road
Stanningley
Leeds LS28 6AT, United Kingdom
+44 (0) 113 255 5665
e-mail: hk@hkeurope.com

Australia: Human Kinetics
57A Price Avenue
Lower Mitcham, South Australia 5062
08 8277 1555
e-mail: liaw@hkaustralia.com

New Zealand: Human Kinetics
Division of Sports Distributors NZ Ltd.
P.O. Box 300 226 Albany
North Shore City
Auckland
0064 9 448 1207
e-mail: info@humankinetics.co.nz

Contents

Welcome to Coaching

Coaching young people is an exciting way to be involved in sport. But it isn't easy. Some coaches are overwhelmed by the responsibilities involved in helping athletes through their early sport experiences. And that's not surprising because coaching youngsters requires more than bringing the balls to the field and letting them play. It also involves preparing them physically and mentally to compete effectively, fairly, and safely in their sport and providing them with a positive role model.

This book will help you meet the challenges and experience the many rewards of coaching young athletes. You'll learn how to meet your responsibilities as a coach, communicate well and provide for safety, and teach tactics and skills while keeping them fun, and you'll learn strategies for coaching on game day. There are 33 drills and games included to help you with your practices. We also provide a sample practice plan and season plan to help guide you throughout your season.

This book serves as a text for the American Sport Education Program's (ASEP) Coaching Youth Football course, official course of USA Football. If you would like more information about this course or other ASEP courses and resources, please contact us at the following address:

ASEP
P.O. Box 5076
Champaign, IL 61825-5076
800-747-5698
www.ASEP.com/coachingyouthfootball

Welcome From USA Football

Dear Coach:

On behalf of USA Football, welcome to *Coaching Youth Football*. This is the first in a series of coaching resources we are developing for youth football coaches. Whether it's learning to teach the proper fundamental skills or better communicate, this book can guide you through your youth football coaching experience.

You will find it to be an easy-to-follow book and an excellent introduction to youth coaching. It provides important information on how to coach a successful team starting with the first day of practice to the final game of the season, while along the way teaching young players valuable skills.

Having played the game of football at every level and having watched my two sons, and now grandsons, come through the ranks as well, I truly understand the value of high-quality coaches and the unique role they play in a young person's life.

This is why a key component of USA Football's mission is helping encourage coaches about their tremendous opportunities and responsibilities for influencing today's youth. Working with the American Sport Education Program (ASEP), our goal is to provide youth coaches with top-quality resources that will help expand their knowledge of the sport, thus helping ensure every coach and every player has a positive experience.

The benefits of coaching last a lifetime, and we are proud of these efforts to encourage our nation's coaches, whose efforts are worthy of praise.

Very Sincerely Yours,
Jack Kemp

Key to Diagrams

Offensive Positions

C	Center
F	Flanker
FB	Fullback
G	Guard
H	Holder
HB	Halfback
K	Kicker
QB	Quarterback
SE	Split end
T	Tackle
TB	Tailback
TE	Tight end
WB	Wingback
WR	Wide receiver

Defensive Positions

CB	Corner back
DE	Defensive end
DT	Defensive tackle
FS	Free safety
LB	Linebacker
MA	Middle linebacker--weak side (Mack)
MI	Middle linebacker (Mike)
S	Outside linebacker--strong side (Sam)
SS	Strong safety
W	Outside linebacker (Will)

Drill Finder

Stepping Into Coaching

I f you are like most youth league coaches, you have probably been recruited from the ranks of concerned parents, sport enthusiasts, or community volunteers. Like many rookie and veteran coaches, you probably have had little formal instruction on how to coach. But when the call went out for coaches to assist with the local youth football program, you answered because you like children and enjoy football and perhaps because you wanted to be involved in a worthwhile community activity.

Your initial coaching assignment may be difficult. Like many volunteers, you may not know everything there is to know about football or about how to work with children. *Coaching Youth Football* presents the basics of coaching football effectively. To start, we look at your responsibilities and what's involved in being a coach. We also talk about what to do when your child is on the team you coach, and we examine five tools for being an effective coach.

Your Responsibilities As a Coach

Coaching at any level involves much more than designing scoring plays for offense or drawing up defenses that keep the other team away from your goal line. Coaching involves accepting the tremendous responsibility you face when parents put their children into your care. As a football coach, you'll be called upon to do the following:

1. *Provide a safe physical environment.*

   Playing football holds inherent risks, but as a coach you're responsible for regularly inspecting the practice and competition fields and equipment (see "Facilities and Equipment Checklist" in appendix A on page 168).

   Make it a priority to explain to the players and parents before the start of the season that football is a contact sport. Therefore, during the course of the year, players

   • will get bumps and bruises,

   • will be tired and need extra rest, and

   • will need to increase their fluid intake to stay hydrated.

   Teach players and parents the importance of keeping their equipment in good working order (see chapter 3 for more information). Reassure them that, to avoid injury, they will learn the safest techniques and that you have a safety game plan and you will follow it (see chapter 4 for more information).

2. *Communicate in a positive way.*

   As you can already see, you have a lot to communicate. You'll communicate not only with your players and parents but also with the coaching staff, officials, administrators, and others. Communicate in a way that is positive and that demonstrates that you have the best interests of the players at heart (see chapter 2 for more information).

3. *Teach the fundamental skills of football.*

   When teaching the fundamental skills of football, keep in mind that football is a game, and as such, you want to be sure that your athletes have fun. Therefore, we ask that you help all players be the best they can be by creating a fun, yet productive, practice environment (see chapter 5 for more information). To help your athletes improve their skills, you need to have a sound understanding of offensive, defensive, and special teams skills (see chapters 6 to 8 for more information).

4. *Teach the rules of football.*

   Introduce the rules of football and incorporate them into individual instruction (see chapter 3 for more information). Many rules can be taught in the first practice, including properly aligning the offense, avoiding illegal procedures, and how to handle being caught offside. Plan to review the rules, however, any time an opportunity naturally arises in practices.

5. *Direct players in competition.*

   This includes determining starting lineup and a substitution plan, relating appropriately to officials and to opposing coaches and players, and making sound tactical decisions during games (see chapter 9 for more information on coaching during games). Remember that the focus is not on winning at all costs but on coaching your kids to compete well, do their best, improve their football skills, and strive to win within the rules.

6. *Help your players become fit and value fitness for a lifetime.*

   We want you to help your players be fit so that they can play football safely and successfully. We also want your players to learn to become fit on their own, understand the value of fitness, and enjoy training. Thus, we ask you not to make them do push-ups or run laps as punishment. Make it fun to get fit for football, and make it fun to play football so that they'll stay fit for a lifetime.

7. *Help young people develop character.*

   Character development includes learning, caring, being honest and respectful, and taking responsibility. These intangible qualities are no

> **Coaching Tip**
> Although it may take more thought and may require you to plan ahead, always explain to parents what you are trying to accomplish as a staff, and explain to players what you want them to do rather than what they should not do.

less important to teach than the skill of blocking well. We ask you to teach these values to players by demonstrating and encouraging behaviors that express these values at all times. For example, in blocking, stress to young players the importance of learning their assignments, helping their teammates, playing within the rules, showing respect for their opponents, and understanding that they are responsible for winning the individual battle on every play even though they may not be recognized individually for their efforts.

These are your responsibilities as a coach. Remember that every player is an individual and you must provide a wholesome environment in which every player has the opportunity to learn how to play the game without fear while having fun and enjoying the overall football experience.

Coaching Your Own Child

Coaching can become even more complicated when your child plays on the team you coach. Many coaches are parents, but the two roles should not be confused. As a parent you are responsible only for yourself and your child, but as a coach you are also responsible for the organization, all the players on the team, and their parents. Because of this additional responsibility, your behavior on the football field will be different from your behavior at home, and your son or daughter may not understand why.

For example, imagine the confusion of a young boy who is the center of his parents' attention at home but is barely noticed by his father (who is also the team coach) in the sport setting. Or consider the mixed signals received by a young girl whose skill is constantly evaluated at practice by a coach (who is also her mother) who otherwise rarely comments on her daughter's activities. You need to explain to your child your new responsibilities and how they will affect your relationship when coaching. Take the following steps to avoid problems when coaching your own child:

- Ask your child if he wants you to coach the team.
- Explain why you want to be involved with the team.
- Discuss with your child how your interactions will change when you take on the role of coach at practices or games.
- Limit your coaching behavior to when you are in the coaching role.
- Avoid parenting during practice or game situations in order to keep your role clear in your child's mind.
- Reaffirm your love for your child, irrespective of his performance on the football field.

Five Tools of an Effective Coach

Have you purchased the traditional coaching tools—things like whistles, coaching clothes, sport shoes, and a clipboard? They'll help you in the act of coaching, but to be successful you'll need five other tools that cannot be bought. These tools are available only through self-examination and hard work; they're easy to remember with the acronym COACH:

C Comprehension

O Outlook

A Affection

C Character

H Humor

Comprehension

Comprehension of the rules, tactics, and skills of football is required. You must understand the elements of the sport. To improve your comprehension of football, take the following steps:

- Read about the rules of football in chapter 3 of this book.
- Read about the fundamentals of football and the football plays in chapters 6 through 8 of this book.
- Read additional football coaching books, including those available from the American Sport Education Program (ASEP).
- Contact youth football organizations, including USA Football (www.usafootball.com).
- Attend football coaching clinics (Coaching Academy Program) and NFL/NFF.
- Talk with more experienced coaches.
- Observe local college, high school, and youth football games.
- Watch football games on television.

In addition to having football knowledge, you must implement proper training and safety methods so that your players can participate with little risk of injury. Even then, injuries may occur. And more often than not, you'll be the first person responding to your players' injuries, so be sure you understand the basic emergency care procedures described in chapter 4. Also, read in that chapter about how to handle more serious sport injuries.

Assessing Your Priorities

Even though all coaches focus on competition, we want you to focus on *positive* competition—keeping the pursuit of victory in perspective by making decisions that, first, are in the best interest of the players, and second, will help to win the game.

So, how do you know if your outlook and priorities are in order? Here's a little test:

1. Which situation would you be most proud of?
   a. *knowing that each participant enjoyed playing football*
   b. *seeing that all players improved their football skills*
   c. *winning the league championship*

2. Which statement best reflects your thoughts about sport?
   a. *If it isn't fun, don't do it.*
   b. *Everyone should learn something every day.*
   c. *Sport isn't fun if you don't win.*

3. How would you like your players to remember you?
   a. *as a coach who was fun to play for*
   b. *as a coach who provided a good base of fundamental skills*
   c. *as a coach who had a winning record*

4. Which would you most like to hear a parent of a player on your team say?
   a. *Mike really had a good time playing football this year.*
   b. *Mike learned some important lessons playing football this year.*
   c. *Mike played on the first-place football team this year.*

5. Which of the following would be the most rewarding moment of your season?
   a. *having your team want to continue playing, even after practice is over*
   b. *seeing one of your players finally master the skill of tackling*
   c. *winning the league championship*

Look over your answers. If you most often selected "a" responses, then having fun is most important to you. A majority of "b" answers suggests that skill development is what attracts you to coaching. And if "c" was your most frequent response, winning is tops on your list of coaching priorities. If your priorities are in order, your players' well-being will take precedence over your team's win-loss record every time.

Outlook

This coaching tool refers to your perspective and goals—what you seek as a coach. The most common coaching objectives are to (a) have fun, (b) help players develop their physical, mental, and social skills, and (c) win. Thus, your outlook involves your priorities, your planning, and your vision for the future. See "Assessing Your Priorities" to learn more about the priorities you set for yourself as a coach.

ASEP has a motto that will help you keep your outlook in line with the best interests of the kids on your team. It summarizes in four words all you need to remember when establishing your coaching priorities:

Athletes First, Winning Second

This motto recognizes that striving to win is an important, even vital, part of sports. But it emphatically states that no efforts in striving to win should be made at the expense of the athletes' well-being, development, and enjoyment.

Take the following actions to better define your outlook:

- With your coaches, determine your priorities for the season.
- Prepare for situations that challenge your priorities.
- Set goals for yourself and your players that are consistent with your priorities.
- Plan how you and your players can best attain your goals.
- Review your goals frequently to be sure that you are staying on track.

Affection

Another vital tool you will want to have in your coaching kit is a genuine concern for the young people you coach. This requires having a passion for kids, a desire to share with them your enjoyment and knowledge of football, and the patience and understanding that allow each player to grow from his involvement in sport.

You can demonstrate your affection and patience in many ways, including the following:

- Make an effort to get to know each player on your team.
- Treat each player as an individual.
- Empathize with players trying to learn new and difficult skills.
- Treat players as you would like to be treated under similar circumstances.
- Control your emotions.

Coaching Tip

When players know and feel that you care for each of them as individuals, they will care about the team and learn to play the game correctly.

- Show your enthusiasm for being involved with your team.
- Keep an upbeat tempo and positive tone in all of your communications.

Character

The fact that you have decided to coach young football players probably means that you think participation in sport is important. But whether or not participation develops character in your players depends as much on you as it does on the sport itself. How can you help your players build character?

Having good character means modeling appropriate behaviors for sport and life. That means more than just saying the right things. What you say and what you do must match. There is no place in coaching for the "Do as I say, not as I do" philosophy. Challenge, support, encourage, and reward every youngster, and your players will be more likely to accept, even celebrate, their differences. Be in control before, during, and after all practices and games. And don't be afraid to admit that you were wrong. No one is perfect!

Each member of your coaching staff should consider the following steps to becoming a good role model:

- Take stock of your strengths and weaknesses.
- Build on your strengths.
- Set goals for yourself to improve on those areas you don't want to see copied.
- If you slip up, apologize to your team and to yourself. You'll do better next time.

Humor

Humor is an often-overlooked coaching tool. For our use, it means having the ability to laugh at yourself and with your players during practices and contests. Nothing helps balance the seriousness of a skill session like a chuckle or two. And a sense of humor puts in perspective the many mistakes your players will make. So don't get upset over each miscue or respond negatively to erring players. Allow your players and yourself to enjoy the ups, and don't dwell on the downs.

Here are some tips for injecting humor into your practices:

- Make practices fun by including a variety of activities.
- Keep all players involved in games and skill practices.
- Consider laughter by your players a sign of enjoyment, not of waning discipline.
- Smile!

2

Communicating
As a Coach

In chapter 1, you learned about the tools you need for coaching: comprehension, outlook, affection, character, and humor. These are essentials for effective coaching; without them, you'd have a difficult time getting started. But none of the tools will work if you don't know how to use them with your athletes—and this requires skillful communication. This chapter examines what communication is and how you can become a more effective communicator.

Coaches often mistakenly believe that communication occurs only when instructing players to do something, but verbal commands are only a small part of the communication process. More than half of what is communicated is done so nonverbally. So remember this when you are coaching: Actions speak louder than words.

Communication in its simplest form involves two people: a sender and a receiver. The sender transmits the message verbally, through facial expressions, and possibly through body language. Once the message is sent, the receiver must receive it and, optimally, understand it. A receiver who fails to pay attention or listen will miss parts, if not all, of the message.

Sending Effective Messages

Young athletes often have little understanding of the rules and skills of football and probably even less confidence in their ability to play it. So they need accurate, understandable, and supportive messages to help them along. That's why your verbal and nonverbal messages are important.

Verbal Messages

"Sticks and stones may break my bones, but words will never hurt me" isn't true. Spoken words can have a strong and long-lasting effect. And coaches' words are particularly influential because youngsters place great importance on what coaches say. Perhaps you, like many former youth sport participants, have a difficult time remembering much of anything you were told by your elementary school teachers, but you can still recall several specific things your coaches at that level said to you. Such is the lasting effect of a coach's comments to a player.

Whether you are correcting misbehavior, teaching a player how to catch the ball, or praising a player for good effort, you should remember several things when sending a message verbally:

- Be positive and honest.
- State it clearly and simply.
- Say it loud enough, and say it again.
- Be consistent.

Be Positive and Honest

Nothing turns people off like hearing someone nag all the time, and athletes react similarly to a coach who gripes constantly. Kids particularly need encouragement because they often doubt their ability to perform in a sport. So look for and tell your players what they did well.

But don't cover up poor or incorrect play with rosy words of praise. Kids know all too well when they've erred, and no cheerfully expressed cliche can undo their mistakes. If you fail to acknowledge players' errors, your athletes will think you are a phony.

An effective way to correct a performance error is to first point out the parts of the technique or tactics that the athlete performed correctly. Then explain—in a positive manner—the error that the player made and show him the correct way to do it. Finish by encouraging the athlete and emphasizing the correct performance.

Be sure not to follow a positive statement with the word "but." For example, you shouldn't say, "Great handoff, Billy, but make certain you carry out your fake after handing the ball to the running back." This causes many kids to ignore the positive statement and focus on the negative one. Instead, say, "Great handoff, Billy. And if you set up after the handoff, the defense will not know it is a run. Also, you will be in a good position to throw our play action pass. Great handoff. Way to go."

State It Clearly and Simply

Positive and honest messages are good, but only if expressed directly in words your players understand. Beating around the bush is ineffective and inefficient. And if you ramble, your players will miss the point of your message and probably lose interest. Here are tips for saying things clearly:

- Organize your thoughts before speaking to your athletes.
- Know your subject as completely as possible.
- Explain things thoroughly, but don't bore your athletes with long-winded monologues.
- Use language your players can understand and be consistent in your terminology. However, avoid trying to be hip by using their age group's slang.

Say It Loud Enough, and Say It Again

Talk to your team in a voice that all members can hear. A crisp, vigorous voice commands attention and respect; garbled and weak speech is tuned out. It's okay and, in fact, appropriate, to soften your voice when speaking to a player individually about a personal problem. But most of the time your messages will be for all your players to hear, so make sure they can! An enthusiastic voice also motivates players and tells them you enjoy being their coach. A word of caution, however: Avoid dominating the setting with a booming voice that detracts attention from players' performances.

Sometimes what you say, even if stated loudly and clearly, won't sink in the first time. This may be particularly true when young athletes hear words they don't understand. To avoid boring repetition and still get your message across, say the same thing in a slightly different way. For instance, you might first tell your players, "Get an angle on the runner." If they don't appear to understand, you might say, "Try to meet and tackle the ball carrier near or behind the line of scrimmage without letting him get by you for a touchdown." The second form of the message may get through to players who missed it the first time around. Remember, terms that you are familiar with and understand may be completely foreign to your players, especially beginning players.

Be Consistent

People often say things in ways that imply a different message. For example, a touch of sarcasm added to the words "Way to go!" sends an entirely different message than the words themselves suggest. Avoid sending mixed messages. Keep the tone of your voice consistent with the words you use. And don't say something one day and contradict it the next; players will get their wires crossed.

You also want to keep your terminology consistent. Many football terms describe the same or similar skill or technique. One coach may use the term "angle block" to describe blocking a defensive player lined up on the line inside of the blocker, while another coach may call the same technique a "down block." Both are correct. To be consistent as a staff, however, agree on all terms before the start of the season and then stay with them (see appendix B beginning on page 179 for common football terms).

Nonverbal Messages

Just as you should be consistent in the tone of voice and words you use, you should also keep your verbal and nonverbal messages consistent. An extreme example of failing to do this would be shaking your head, indicating disapproval, while at the same time telling a player, "Nice try." Which is the player to believe, your gesture or your words?

Messages can be sent nonverbally in several ways. Facial expressions and body language are just two of the more obvious forms of nonverbal signals that can help you when you coach. Keep in mind that as a coach you need to be a teacher first, and any action that detracts from the message you are trying to convey to your players should be avoided.

Coaching Tip
Calm and controlled actions and voice allow players to focus on your message rather than on what your personal feelings may be.

Facial Expressions

The look on a person's face is the quickest clue to what he or she thinks or feels. Your players know this, so they will study your face, looking for a sign that will tell them more than the words you say. Don't try to fool them by putting on a happy or blank "mask." They'll see through it, and you'll lose credibility.

Serious, stone-faced expressions provide no cues to kids who want to know how they are performing. When faced with this, kids will just assume you're unhappy or disinterested. Don't be afraid to smile. A smile from a coach can give a great boost to an unsure athlete. Plus, a smile lets your players know that you are happy to be coaching them. But don't overdo it, or your players won't be able to tell when you are genuinely pleased by something they've done or when you are just putting on a smiling face.

Body Language

What would your players think you were feeling if you came to practice slouched over with your head down and shoulders slumped? You were tired, bored, or unhappy? What would they think you were feeling if you watched them during a contest with your hands on your hips, your jaws clenched, and your face reddened? You were upset with them, disgusted at an official, or mad at a fan? Probably some or all of these things would enter your players' minds. And none is the impression you want your players to have of you. That's why you should carry yourself in a pleasant, confident, and vigorous manner. This posture not only projects happiness with your coaching role but also provides a good example for your young players who may model your behavior.

> **Coaching Tip**
> Avoid wild hand gestures or standing with crossed arms or with your hands in your pockets when coaching at a practice or a game. These postures can cause players to feel that you do not care or are upset with or are indifferent to the actions of the team.

Physical contact can also be a very important use of body language. A handshake, a pat on the head, an arm around the shoulder, or even a big hug are effective ways to show approval, concern, affection, and joy to your players. Youngsters are especially in need of this type of nonverbal message. Keep within the obvious moral and legal limits, of course, but don't be reluctant to touch your players, sending a message that can only be expressed in that way.

Improving Your Receiving Skills

Now, let's examine the other half of the communication process: receiving messages. Too often, very good senders are very poor receivers of messages. But as a coach of young athletes, you must be able to fulfill both roles effectively.

The requirements for receiving messages are quite simple, but receiving skills are perhaps less satisfying and therefore underdeveloped compared to sending skills. People seem to enjoy hearing themselves talk more than they enjoy hearing others talk. But if you learn the keys to receiving messages and make a strong effort to use them with your players, you'll be surprised by what you've been missing.

Pay Attention

First, you must pay attention; you must want to hear what others have to communicate to you. That's not always easy when you're busy coaching and have many things competing for your attention. But in one-on-one or team meetings with players, you must focus on what they are telling you, both verbally and nonverbally. Make certain to establish and maintain good eye contact. You'll be amazed at the little signals you pick up. Not only will this focused attention help you catch every word your players say, but also you'll notice your players' moods and physical states. In addition, you'll get an idea of your players' feelings toward you and other players on the team.

Listen Carefully

How we receive messages from others, perhaps more than anything else we do, demonstrates how much we care for the sender and what that person has to tell us. If you care little for your players or have little regard for what they have to say, it will show in how you attend and listen to them. Check yourself. Do you find your mind wandering to what you are going to do after practice while one of your players is talking to you? Do you frequently have to ask your players, "What did you say?" If so, you need to work on your receiving mechanics of attending and listening. But perhaps the most critical question you should ask yourself, if you find that you're missing the messages your players send, is this: "Do I care?"

Providing Feedback

So far we've discussed sending and receiving messages separately. But we all know that senders and receivers switch roles several times during an interaction. One person initiates a communication by sending a message to another person, who then receives the message. The receiver then becomes the sender by responding to the person who sent the initial message. These verbal and nonverbal responses are called feedback.

Your players will look to you for feedback all the time. They will want to know how you think they are performing, what you think of their ideas, and whether their efforts please you. You can respond in many different ways, and how you respond will strongly affect your players. They will react most favorably to positive feedback.

Praising players when they perform or behave well is an effective way to get them to repeat (or try to repeat) that behavior. And positive feedback for effort is an especially effective way to motivate youngsters to work on difficult skills. So rather than shouting at and providing negative feedback to players who have made mistakes, try offering positive feedback and letting them know what they did correctly and how they can improve. Sometimes the way you word feedback can make it more positive than negative. For example, instead of saying, "Don't run with the ball that way," you might say, "Run with the ball this way." Then your players will focus on what to do instead of what not to do.

Positive feedback can be verbal or nonverbal. Telling young players, especially in front of teammates, that they have performed well is a great way to boost their confidence. And a pat on the back or a handshake communicates that you recognize a player's performance.

Communicating With Others

Coaching involves not only sending and receiving messages and providing proper feedback to players but also interacting with members of the staff, parents, fans, contest officials, and opposing coaches. If you don't communicate effectively with these groups, your coaching career will be unpleasant and short lived. So try the following suggestions for communicating with these groups.

Coaching Staff

Before you hold your first practice, it is important for the coaching staff to meet and discuss the roles and responsibilities that each coach will undertake during the year. Depending on the number of assistant coaches, the staff responsibilities can be divided into a head coach; offensive, defensive, and special teams coordinators; a conditioning coach; and various position coaches. The head coach has the final responsibility for all phases of the game, but, as much as possible, area coaches should be responsible for their groups.

Each coordinator will be responsible for his or her area. During games, under the direction of the head coach, the coordinator will call the plays for the team on the field.

Before practices start, the coaching staff must also discuss and agree on terminology, plans for practice, schemes, game-day organization, and the method of communicating during practice and game conditions. The coaches on your staff must present a united front and speak with one voice, and they must all take a similar approach to coaching, interaction with the players and parents, and interactions with one another. Discussions of disagreements should be conducted away from the playing field where each coach can have a say and the staff can come to an agreement.

Coaching Tip

As a head coach, enlist assistant coaches who work together and bring unique strengths to your staff. Avoid the trap of coaches who only mirror the strengths you bring to the team.

Parents

A player's parents need to be assured that their son is under the direction of a coach who is both knowledgeable about the sport and concerned about their youngster's well-being. You can put their worries to rest by holding a preseason parent orientation meeting in which you describe your background and your approach to coaching (see "Preseason Meeting Topics").

Preseason Meeting Topics

1. Outline paperwork that is needed:
   - Copy of player's birth certificate
   - Completed player's application and payment record
   - Report card from the previous year
   - Participation agreement form
   - Informed consent form

2. Go over the inherent risks of football and other safety issues.

3. Inform parents of uniform and equipment handout date and time.

4. Review the season practice schedule including date, location, and time of each practice.

5. Go over proper conditioning attire for the first days of practice, including accessories.

6. Designate certification day and list weight limits for players.

7. Discuss nutrition, hydration, and rest for players.

8. Explain goals for the team.

9. Cover methods of communication: e-mail list, emergency phone numbers, interactive Web site, and so on.

10. Discuss ways that parents can help with the team.

11. Discuss standards of conduct for coaches, players, and parents.

12. Provide time for questions and answers.

If parents contact you with a concern during the season, listen to them closely and try to offer positive responses. If you need to communicate with parents, catch them after a practice, phone them, or send a note through e-mail or the U.S. mail. Messages sent to parents through players are too often lost, misinterpreted, or forgotten.

Fans

The stands probably won't be overflowing at your contests, which means that you'll more easily hear the few fans who criticize your coaching. When you hear something negative about the job you're doing, don't respond. Keep calm, consider whether the message has any value, and if not, forget it. Acknowledging critical, unwarranted comments from a fan during a contest will only encourage others to voice their opinions. So put away your "rabbit ears," and communicate to fans, through your actions, that you are a confident, competent coach.

Prepare your players, too, for fans' criticism. Tell them it is you, not the spectators, they should listen to. If you notice that one of your players is rattled by a fan's comment, reassure the player that your evaluation is more objective and favorable—and the one that counts.

Officials

How you communicate with officials will greatly influence the way your players behave toward them. Therefore, you must set an example. Greet officials with a handshake, an introduction, and perhaps casual conversation about the upcoming contest. Indicate your respect for them before, during, and after the game. Don't make nasty remarks, shout, or use disrespectful body gestures. Your players will see you do it, and they'll get the idea that such behavior is appropriate. Plus, if the official hears or sees you, communication between the two of you will break down.

Opposing Coaches

Make an effort to visit with the coach of the opposing team before the game. During the game, don't get into a personal feud with the opposing coach. Remember, it's the kids, not the coaches, who are competing. And by getting along well with the opposing coach, you show your players that competition involves cooperation.

3

Understanding Rules and Equipment

ootball is a complicated game played by large teams divided into numerous positions, all governed by a thick rule book. This introduction to the basic rules of football won't cover every rule of the game but instead will give you what you need to work with players who are 8 to 14 years old. This chapter covers terminology, field size and markings, ball size, and equipment. It also describes player positions and game procedures and scoring, reviews the rules of play, and wraps things up with officiating and some of the officiating signals.

Field

Most youth programs play on regulation high school fields, but some may play on fields with 80 yards between goal lines and 40 yards between sidelines (see figure 3.1). Some programs start players on even smaller 60-yard by 30-yard fields. Stadiums may be different, but all fields are defined by the following:

- End lines and sidelines as the outer boundaries of the playing field
- A 10-yard end zone at both ends of the field used for scoring
- A goal line at which any player who is on, above, or over the opponent's goal line scores
- Yard line markers and hash marks between the goal lines
- A goalpost used for field goals and points after touchdowns

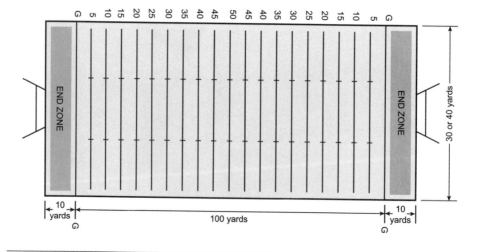

Figure 3.1   Regulation football field.

Football

Just as the size of the field is reduced to match players' development, so too is the size of the ball (see examples shown in tables 3.1a and 3.1b). Your league will probably distribute to all teams a certain size and brand of ball to use throughout the season. The football should have a set of laces and a leather surface is recommended. Check the air pressure of the inflated rubber bladder inside to make sure it is the same as the pressure designated on the ball's exterior.

Any junior- or youth-size ball is allowed. The smaller size lets players learn the proper techniques for throwing and carrying a football at an earlier age.

Table 3.1a   Age-Group Divisions and Ball Dimensions for Pop Warner Football

Age group	Division	Football dimensions (in)
7-9	Mighty Mites	10 1/4-10 1/2
8-10	Junior Pee Wees	10 1/4-10 1/2
9-11	Pee Wees	10 1/4-10 1/2
10-12	Junior Midgets	10 5/8-10 3/4
11-13	Midgets	10 5/8-10 3/4
12-14	Junior Bantams	10 5/8-10 3/4
14	Bantams	11-11 1/2 (regulation)

Table 3.1b   Age-Group Divisions and Ball Dimensions for American Youth Football

Age group	Division	Football dimensions (in)
7-9	Mighty Mites	10 1/4-10 1/2 pee wee ball
8-10	Junior Pee Wees	Junior ball
9-11	Pee Wees	Junior ball
10-12	Junior Midgets	10 5/8-10 3/4 youth ball
11-13	Midgets	Youth ball
12-14	Junior Bantams	11-11 1/2 (regulation)
14	Bantams	11-11 1/2 (regulation)

Player Equipment

The physical nature of football requires that players wear protective gear. These items include a helmet, mouth guard, shoulder pads, girdle pads, thigh pads, knee pads, and cleated shoes.

Examine the condition of each item you distribute to players. Also make sure that the pieces of equipment they furnish themselves meet acceptable standards. In addition, it is important that each piece of equipment is fit to the player. Make sure that each athlete on your team is outfitted properly. To properly fit equipment to a player, see "Player Equipment Checklist" on page 170 in appendix A.

You may have to demonstrate to players how to put on each piece of equipment. Otherwise, expect some of them to show up for the first practice with their shoulder pads on backward and their thigh pads upside down.

Shaping a mouth guard is also a mystery to most youngsters. Although these plastic mouthpieces come with easy-to-follow directions, your players may need further guidance. Take time to explain the heating and shaping process to their parents at the preseason meeting (see "Preseason Meeting Topics" on page 16).

The helmet is the most commonly misused piece of football equipment. So before distributing helmets to your players, explain very clearly that a helmet is a protective covering, not a weapon. If you spot players using their helmet as a battering device, take them aside and demonstrate the correct, heads-up technique, as shown in figure 7.4 on page 108.

Player Positions

Give your young athletes a chance to play a variety of positions, on both offense and defense, and then see where each player can best contribute on special teams. By playing different positions, they'll be provided a better all-around playing experience and will probably stay more interested in the sport. Furthermore, they'll have a better understanding of the many technical skills and tactics used in the game. They will also better appreciate the efforts of their teammates who play positions they find difficult.

Following are descriptions of the offensive, defensive, and special teams positions for football.

Offensive Positions

The offensive team is responsible for moving the football down the field. It typically consists of 11 players, as in the split formation shown in figure 3.2, and is broken down into the following three segments:

1. The offensive linemen who block
2. The receivers who block and catch passes

3. The offensive backfield, which includes the running backs who carry the ball on running plays and act as receivers and blockers and the quarterback who calls the plays, calls the cadence at the line of scrimmage to start the play, takes the ball from the center, and delivers the ball to running backs or throws passes to receivers

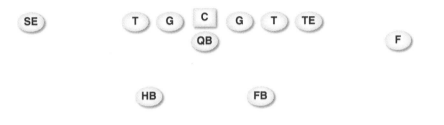

Figure 3.2   Offensive team alignment (split formation).

Following are the basic offensive positions with a short discussion of the skills and duties of each. Refer to chapter 6 for more information on the offense.

Offensive Linemen

Ideally, you'll put big, strong, and quick athletes into the center, guard, and tackle positions. These players must block and open up holes for ball carriers to run through. When a pass play is called, they must protect the quarterback from opposing linemen.

Receivers

Another player who has important blocking duties is the tight end, a receiver positioned on the line of scrimmage next to (within 3 yards of) either tackle. The tight end must be strong enough to block a defensive end or linebacker yet speedy enough to get open on pass routes.

The two other receiver positions are the flanker and the split end, or wide receiver. Speed and agility, along with great catching ability, are the qualities to look for in filling these spots. The flanker can be positioned on either side of the line of scrimmage, whereas the split end is 8 to 10 yards up on the line and outside the tackle opposite the side of the tight end. The flanker is referred to as the slot when lined up on the same side as the split end.

Quarterback

Lined up directly behind the center to receive the snap, the quarterback is the field general of the offense. The quarterback calls the plays in the huddle, barks out the snap count at the line of scrimmage, and then, after taking the snap, hands the ball off, runs with it, or passes it. At this position you want a good communicator and good athlete who can handle many responsibilities. To complete your wish list, the quarterback will have an excellent throwing arm.

Running Backs

Most teams use a two-back set, either a split-back formation like the one shown in figure 3.2 or an I-formation, as shown in figure 3.3, in which the backs line up in a straight line behind the quarterback.

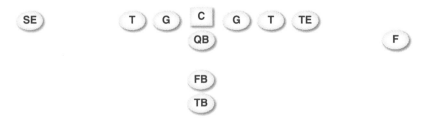

Figure 3.3 I-formation.

Often, one running back is called a fullback and the other a halfback. The fullback has more blocking responsibilities and is expected to pick up short yardage when needed. Therefore, you want a strong, fairly fast, and dependable player at this position. The halfback (called the tailback in the I-formation) is the primary ball carrier. Speed and agility to outrun and outmaneuver would-be tacklers are desirable attributes for a halfback.

Some coaches prefer to line up their teams in a three-back set, moving the flanker to a wing back in the wing-T formation as shown in figure 3.4 or to a second halfback position to form a wishbone formation as shown in figure 3.5. Coaches typically use the wing-T and wishbone formations when they want their team to run the ball much more than pass it.

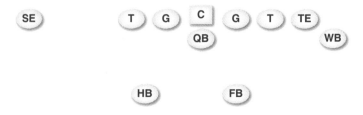

Figure 3.4 Wing-T formation.

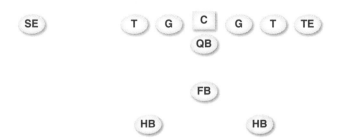

Figure 3.5 Wishbone formation.

Defensive Positions

The defensive players stop the opposing team from moving the football. Defenses are usually called using a two-digit number. The first number tells the number of defensive linemen in the game and the second number designates the number of linebackers. Calling defenses can range from a 3-4 defense to a 7-1 defense and all the variations in between, but youth coaches typically use a 4-3 defense as shown in figure 3.6. Following are the basic defensive positions with a short discussion of the skills and duties of each. For further information on coaching the defense, refer to chapter 7.

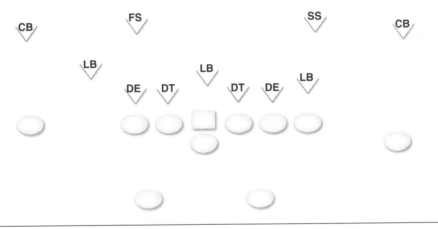

Figure 3.6   4-3 defensive-team alignment.

Defensive Linemen

Youth football coaches put four to six players up front on the line. The four-man front consists of two tackles and two ends. The five-man front adds a nose guard in the middle; the six-man front adds two ends, who may line up in an upright position much like outside linebackers (as discussed in the next section).

Defensive tackles and defensive ends are primarily responsible for defeating the offensive blocker, finding the ball carrier, and then tackling him before he can gain yardage. It is also their duty to rush the passer when the offense attempts to throw the ball. To carry out their assignments, defensive linemen need adequate size and strength as well as great quickness to fend off or avoid blocks by offensive players.

Linebackers

You want two to four linebackers on defense, depending on the number of linemen you use. No matter how many you use, each should have a nose for the ball—that is, be able to read the offense's play and stop it quickly.

The standard 4-3 defense with a three-linebacker set, as shown in figure 3.6, complements the four-man front nicely. In this alignment, you have a middle linebacker at the heart of the defense and two outside linebackers.

The middle linebacker should be one of your best athletes and surest tacklers. The outside linebacker on the tight end side, often called "Sam" to indicate that he plays on the offense's strong side, must be strong enough to fend off blocks but also fast enough to cover the tight end on pass routes. "Will," the name often used when referring to the weak-side linebacker, must be able to stand his ground against blocks by linemen and backs to prevent the offense from running the ball successfully. This linebacker must also have the range to drop into zone coverage to the side of the split end.

Defensive Backs

The players responsible for preventing long runs and completed passes by the offense are the defensive backs. Again, depending on the alignment of your defensive front, the offense's set, and the game situation, you will have three to five defensive backs in the game. Safeties have run-and-pass responsibilities. Cornerbacks cover the wide-outs on many pass coverages but have to come up to play a running play to their side when the team is using a two-deep pass coverage.

All of these players must be agile and fast so that they can cover speedy receivers. And the safeties must be good tacklers in order to help linebackers stop the run.

Special Teams Positions

Besides assigning players to the basic offensive and defensive spots, you will designate players for special teams positions. "Special teams" refers to all members of the football team who participate in the kicking game. This includes the players involved in kicking the ball—the punt, kickoff, and field goal and point-after-touchdown (PAT) teams; the players that return the punt—the return and kickoff return teams; and the players that block the kick—the field goal and PAT block teams.

Following is a quick look at the key positions for each team. For further information on special teams, refer to chapter 8.

Punt, Kickoff, and Field Goal and PAT Teams

The players on these teams are involved in the kicking phase of the game and must be taught the basic skills of blocking and tackling. They also must learn how to run down the field to cover the kick. These three teams also require the following specific players—or specialists—with additional specialized skills:

- *Short snapper:* Player who centers the ball back 7 yards to the holder on the field goal and PAT team, referred to as center on field goal team
- *Long snapper:* Player who centers the ball back to the punter, who can be lined up 10 to 15 yards behind the long snapper depending on the ability of the long snapper, referred to as center on punt team
- *Holder:* Player who receives the snap on field goal attempts and places the ball on the tee for the kicker, referred to as holder on field goal and PAT team

- *Kicker:* Player who kicks the ball off the tee during the kickoff, referred to as kicker on kickoff and field goal and PAT team
- *Punter:* Player who punts the ball, referred to as punter on punt team

Punt and Kickoff Return Teams

Punt and kickoff return teams receive the punt or kickoff and try to move the ball down the field to gain advantageous field position for their offensive team. All of these players must learn the basic skill of blocking. These two teams also require the following specific players—or specialists—with additional specialized skills:

- *Kick returner:* Player on the kickoff return team who is farthest from the kicker and ideally is the player who fields and runs with the ball; also referred to as kickoff returner
- *Punt returner:* Player on the punt return team who is farthest from the punter and ideally is the player who fields and runs with the ball

How the Game Is Played

The game of football begins with a kickoff. A player on one team kicks the ball from a designated yard line off a tee toward the opponent's goal line. A player on either team can gain possession of the ball after it travels 10 yards downfield. If, as usually happens, a player on the receiving team gains possession, that player tries to advance the ball as far as possible toward the kicking team's goal line. The kicking team tries to tackle the ball carrier, as close to the receiving team's goal as possible. When the returner is tackled or the ball carrier runs out of bounds, the officials whistle the ball dead and momentarily stop play.

The point where play resumes is called the line of scrimmage. The line of scrimmage stretches from one sideline to the other, passing through the point of the ball nearest the defense. The team with the ball is the offense; the opposing team is the defense. In 11-man football, the offensive team must begin each play with at least seven players lined up on the line of scrimmage, facing the defense. Each play starts when one of these linemen—the center—snaps the ball to a teammate, typically the quarterback.

The offense is allowed four plays—or downs—to advance the football 10 yards toward the opponent's goal line. If successful, the offense is given a new set of downs and can maintain possession until it

- is stopped by the defense and has to punt, typically on fourth down;
- turns the ball over to the defense by means of a fumble, interception, or failure to gain 10 yards in four attempts;
- attempts a field goal; or
- scores a touchdown.

Scoring

The primary objective of the offensive team is to score, although many coaches also want their offense to maintain possession of the ball for as long as possible. By doing so they reduce the number of chances the opposing team's offense has to score.

The defensive team's main objective is to prevent the offense from scoring. In addition, the defense tries to make the offensive team give up possession of the ball as far as possible from the goal line it is defending.

Many strategic options to accomplish these objectives are available to offenses and defenses. Read chapters 6 and 7 for information on how to teach your team basic offensive and defensive plays.

Rules of Play

Football rules are designed to make the game run smoothly and safely and prevent either team from gaining an unfair advantage. Throw out the rules, and a football game quickly turns into a chaotic and dangerous competition where size, brute strength, and speed dominate.

Your league should already have rules concerning acceptable height and weight maximums and minimums for players. Even so, make sure your kids are matched up against opponents with similar physiques and skills. Discourage players from cutting weight to be eligible for your team and, if you spot a mismatch during a game, talk with the opposing coach to see if you can cooperate and correct the problem.

Your league will also specify the length of your games. Typically, youth football games consist of four 8- or 10-minute quarters. The clock is stopped when

- there is a change of possession,
- the ball goes out of bounds,
- an incomplete pass is thrown,
- the yard markers need to be advanced after a team gains 10 yards for a first down,
- a player is injured and officials call a time-out,
- a team scores, or
- a team calls a time-out.

You will be given two or three time-outs in each half. Use them wisely, not just for talking strategy. Remember, although the games may seem short to you, young players can easily become fatigued. So, besides substituting regularly, call a time-out when you see that your team is tired.

Rule Infractions

Pop Warner football, American Youth Football, and your local youth football program have rule books available for your use. Study them, learn the ins and outs, and then teach the rules to your football team.

Although no youth football team will perform penalty free, teach your players to avoid recurring penalties. For example, if a penalty occurs in practice, stop the play and briefly discuss the result of the penalty. By instilling this discipline, you'll help players enjoy more success, both as individuals and as a team.

Here is a brief list of common infractions that football players commit:

- *Offside:* Defensive player in or beyond the neutral zone when the ball is snapped
- *Encroachment:* Offensive player in or beyond the neutral zone before the ball is snapped
- *Illegal formation or false start:* Failure of the offensive team to have seven players on the line of scrimmage (in 11-man football); the offensive team having more than one player in motion or a player moving toward the line of scrimmage before the snap
- *Delay of game:* Offensive team taking more than 25 seconds to snap the ball after the referee has marked it ready for play
- *Holding:* Any player using the arms to hook or lock up an opponent to impede his movement; an offensive player extending the arms outside the body frame to grab an opponent
- *Pass interference (defensive):* Defensive player making contact with an eligible receiver who is beyond the neutral zone with the intent of impeding the offensive player trying to catch a catchable forward pass

As you teach your athletes to play with discipline and to avoid these rule violations, remember that you are their model. Players will reflect the discipline that you display in teaching them in practices and coaching them from the sidelines during games. So show respect for the rules, and don't shrug off game infractions or personal misconduct. And provide a great example by communicating respectfully with the individuals who officiate your games.

Playing by the Rules

You are in a position to teach your players more than simply obeying the rules of the game. As a coach, you have a responsibility to teach them only those techniques that are safe.

For example, you must discourage spearing on defense because it's against the rules. But it's also essential to teach young players never to lead with their heads when blocking or running. Kicking or striking an opponent or jumping on the pile at the conclusion of a play is not acceptable. Also, teach your players not to grasp an opponent's face mask because doing so can cause serious neck injuries. If you fail to teach and enforce these rules, you are directly contributing not only to the next penalty one of your players commits, but also to the next injury one of your players suffers.

Football is a contact, perhaps collision, sport. If participants play according to the letter and spirit of the rules, they can participate safely. Make certain that your players do. Proper football techniques for young football players are described in chapters 6, 7, and 8. Refer to "Football No-Nos" for a list of the techniques that you should not tolerate.

Football No-Nos

It's inevitable that your players will violate minor rules during practices and games; even pros go offside now and then. But make clear to your players that some actions are unacceptable on the football field. Officials typically call unsportsmanlike-conduct penalties or personal fouls for these actions:

- Tripping
- Face mask (grabbing an opponent's face mask)
- Blocking or tackling with a closed fist
- Spearing (tackling with the top of the helmet)
- Swearing
- Taunting
- Fighting
- Clipping (blocking a player in the back)
- Clotheslining (knocking a player down with a blow to the head or neck)

Promote good sportsmanship along with the use of proper fundamentals. Encourage players to help opponents up from the ground after a play. Ask ball carriers to hand the ball to the referee or leave it on the ground where they were stopped. The official will appreciate this behavior and so will the players' parents, league administrators, and players' future coaches.

Officiating

Football rules are enforced by a crew of officials on the field. In youth football, as many as seven officials or as few as two may work the games. Referees are the officials who control the game, marking the ball ready for play; signal penalties, time-outs, and first downs; and communicate with team captains and coaches. See figure 3.7, a through n, for common officiating signals.

If you have a concern about how a game is being officiated, address the referees respectfully. Do so immediately if at any time you feel that the officiating jeopardizes the safety of your players.

(continued)

Figure 3.7   Officiating signal for: *(a)* time-out, *(b)* touchdown or field goal, *(c)* personal foul, *(d)* illegal use of hands, *(e)* illegal contact, *(f)* delay of game, *(g)* offside or encroaching, *(h)* holding.

Figure 3.7 *(continued) (i)* illegal motion, *(j)* first down, *(k)* pass interference, *(l)* incomplete pass, penalty refused, or missed kick, *(m)* failure to wear required equipment, and *(n)* roughing kicker or holder.

Providing for Players' Safety

Your fullback breaks free through a huge hole in the line, and he appears to have daylight all the way to the end zone. Suddenly, a linebacker comes from nowhere and makes a crushing tackle on the runner. Although momentarily pleased with the yardage gained on the play, you quickly become concerned when you see that the ball carrier is not getting to his feet. He seems to be in pain. What do you do?

No coach wants to see players get hurt. But injury remains a reality of sport participation; consequently, you must be prepared to provide first aid when injuries occur and to protect yourself against unjustified lawsuits. Fortunately, coaches can institute many preventive measures to reduce the risk. In this chapter we describe steps you can take to prevent injuries, first aid and emergency responses for when injuries occur, and your legal responsibilities as a coach.

Game Plan for Safety

You can't prevent all injuries from happening, but you can take preventive measures that give your players the best possible chance for injury-free participation. In creating the safest possible environment for your athletes, you must address these areas:

- Preseason physical examination
- Physical conditioning
- Equipment and facilities inspection
- Player matchups and inherent risks
- Proper supervision and record keeping
- Environmental conditions

Preseason Physical Examination

We recommend that your players have a physical examination before participating in football. The exam should address the most likely areas of medical concern and identify youngsters at high risk. We also suggest that you have players' parents or guardians sign a participation agreement form and an informed consent form to allow their children to be treated in case of an emergency. For a sample form, please see "Informed Consent Form" on page 169 of appendix A.

Physical Conditioning

Players need to be in or get in shape to play the game at the level expected. They must have adequate cardiorespiratory fitness and muscular fitness.

Cardiorespiratory fitness refers to the body's ability to use oxygen and fuels efficiently to power muscle contractions. As players get in better shape, their bodies are able to more efficiently deliver oxygen to fuel muscles and carry off carbon dioxide and other wastes. Football requires lots of running and exertion, usually in short bursts, throughout a game. Youngsters who aren't as fit as their peers often overextend in trying to keep up, which can result in lightheadedness, nausea, fatigue, and potential injury.

Try to remember that the players' goals are to participate, learn, and have fun. Therefore, you must keep the players active, attentive, and involved with every phase of practice. If you do, they will attain higher levels of cardiorespiratory fitness as the season progresses simply by taking part in practice. However, watch closely for signs of low cardiorespiratory fitness; don't let your athletes do much until they're fit. You might privately counsel youngsters who appear overly winded, suggesting that they train under proper supervision outside of practice to increase their fitness.

Muscular fitness encompasses strength, muscular endurance, power, speed, and flexibility. This type of fitness is affected by physical maturity, as well as strength training and other types of training. Your team members will likely exhibit a relatively wide range of muscular fitness. Those who have greater muscular fitness will be able to run faster, jump higher, and throw farther. They will also sustain fewer muscular injuries, and any injuries that do occur will tend to be minor. And in case of injury, recovery is faster in those with higher levels of muscular fitness.

Two other components of fitness and injury prevention are the warm-up and the cool-down. Although young bodies are generally very limber, they too can become tight through inactivity. The warm-up should address each muscle group and elevate the heart rate in preparation for strenuous activity. Players should warm up for 5 to 10 minutes using a combination of light running, jumping, and stretching. As practice winds down, slow players' heart rate with an easy jog or walk. Then have players stretch for 5 minutes to help prevent tight muscles before the next practice or contest.

Equipment and Facilities Inspection

Another way to prevent injuries is to check the quality and fit of uniforms, practice attire, and protective equipment used by your players. Slick-soled, poor-fitting, or unlaced football shoes are a knee or ankle injury waiting to happen. Make sure your players' shoes have appropriately sized studs, are the proper size for their feet, and are double tied to prevent self-inflicted "shoe-string tackles." Two pairs of socks are better than one for preventing blisters.

The pants, pads, jerseys, and helmets your players wear will probably be supplied by your local youth sport program. Check the quality of all equipment and uniforms before fitting them to the kids on your team. After distributing properly fitting equipment that is safe and in good condition, show players how to put on every part of their uniform. Advise them to wear an undershirt, such as a wick-away shirt beneath their shoulder pads to reduce the chance of skin irritations.

Make certain that each player on the field has a mouthpiece in place at all times. And tell your athletes that chin straps should be fastened at all times.

Remember also to examine regularly the field on which your players practice and play. Remove hazards, report conditions you cannot remedy, and request maintenance as necessary. If unsafe conditions exist, either make adaptations to prevent risk to your players' safety or stop the practice or game until safe conditions have been restored. Refer to appendix A for the "Facilities and Equipment Checklist" on page 168 and the "Player Equipment Checklist" on page 170 for forms to guide you in verifying that the facility and player equipment are safe.

Player Matchups and Inherent Risks

We recommend that you group teams in two-year age increments if possible. You'll encounter fewer mismatches in physical maturation with narrow age ranges. Even so, two 12-year-old boys might differ by 90 pounds in weight, a foot in height, and three or four years in emotional and intellectual maturity. This presents dangers for the less mature. Whenever possible, match players against opponents of similar size and physical maturity. This approach gives smaller, less mature youngsters a better chance to succeed and avoid injury while providing more mature players with a greater challenge. Closely supervise games so that the more mature players do not put the less mature players at undue risk.

Although proper matching helps protect you from certain liability concerns, you must also warn players of the inherent risks involved in playing football, because "failure to warn" is one of the most successful arguments in lawsuits against coaches. So, thoroughly explain the inherent risks of football and make sure each player and their parents know, understand, and appreciate those risks. Some of these inherent risks were outlined in chapter 1; learn more about them by talking with your league administrators.

The preseason parent orientation meeting is a good opportunity to explain the risks of the sport to parents and players and then have both the players and their parents sign waivers releasing you from liability should an injury occur. These waivers should be legally reviewed prior to presentation to parents. These waivers do not relieve you of responsibility for your players' well-being, but they are recommended by lawyers and may help you in the event of a lawsuit.

Proper Supervision and Record Keeping

To ensure players' safety, you must provide both general supervision and specific supervision. General supervision means that you are in the area of activity so that you can see and hear what is happening. You should be

- on the field and in position to supervise the players even before the formal practice begins,
- immediately accessible to the activity and able to oversee the entire activity,
- alert to conditions that may be dangerous to players and ready to take action to protect players,
- able to react immediately and appropriately to emergencies, and
- present on the field until the last player has been picked up after the practice or a game.

Specific supervision is the direct supervision of an activity at practice. For example, you should provide specific supervision when you teach new skills and continue it until your athletes understand the requirements of the activity, the risks involved, and their own ability to perform in light of these risks. You also must provide specific supervision when you notice either players breaking rules or a change in the condition of your athletes. As a general rule, the more dangerous the activity, the more specific the supervision required. This suggests that more specific supervision is required with younger and less experienced athletes.

As part of your supervision duty, you are expected to foresee potentially dangerous situations and to be positioned to help prevent them. This requires that you know football well, especially the rules that are intended to provide for safety. Prohibit dangerous horseplay, and hold practices only under safe weather conditions. These specific supervisory activities, applied consistently, will make the play environment safer for your players and will help protect you from liability if a mishap occurs.

For further protection, keep records of your season plans, practice plans, and players' injuries. Season and practice plans come in handy when you need evidence that players have been taught certain skills, whereas accurate, detailed injury report forms offer protection against unfounded lawsuits. Ask for these forms from your sponsoring organization (see page 171 in appendix A for a sample injury report form), and hold onto these records for several years so that an "old football injury" of a former player doesn't come back to haunt you.

Environmental Conditions

Most health problems caused by environmental factors are related to excessive heat or cold, although you should also consider other environmental factors such as severe weather and air pollution. A little thought about potential problems and a little effort to ensure adequate protection for your athletes will prevent most serious emergencies related to environmental conditions.

Coaching Tip

Encourage players to drink plenty of water before, during, and after practice. Water makes up 45 to 65 percent of a youngster's body weight, and even a small amount of water loss can cause severe consequences in the body's systems. It doesn't have to be hot and humid for players to become dehydrated, nor is thirst an accurate indicator of dehydration. In fact, by the time players are aware of their thirst, they are long overdue for a drink.

Heat

On hot, humid days the body has difficulty cooling itself. Because the air is already saturated with water vapor (humidity), sweat doesn't evaporate as easily. Therefore, body sweat is a less effective cooling agent, and the body retains extra heat. Hot, humid environments put athletes at risk of heat exhaustion and heatstroke (see more on these in "Serious Injuries" on pages 45-46). And if *you* think it's hot or humid, it's worse for the kids, not only because they're more active, but also because kids younger than 12 have more difficulty regulating their body temperature than adults do. To provide for players' safety in hot or humid conditions, take the following preventive measures:

- Monitor weather conditions and adjust practices accordingly. Table 4.1 shows the specific air temperatures and humidity percentages that can be hazardous.

- Acclimatize players exercising in high heat and humidity by first training without pads and adding them slowly to help reduce the risk of heat illness. Athletes can adjust to high heat and humidity in 7 to 10 days. During this period, hold practices at low to moderate activity levels and give the players fluid breaks every 20 minutes.

- Switch to light clothing. Players should wear shorts and white T-shirts.

- Identify and monitor players who are prone to heat illness. Players who are overweight, heavily muscled, or out of shape or players who work excessively hard or have suffered previous heat illness are more prone to heat illness. Closely monitor these athletes and give them water breaks every 15 to 20 minutes.

- Make sure athletes replace fluids lost through sweat. Encourage players to drink 17 to 20 ounces of fluid two to three hours before practice or games, 7 to 10 ounces every 20 minutes during practice and after prac-

Table 4.1   Warm-Weather Precautions

Temperature (°F)	Humidity	Precautions
80-90	<70%	Monitor athletes prone to heat illness
80-90	>70%	5-minute rest after 30 minutes of practice
90-100	<70%	5-minute rest after 30 minutes of practice
90-100	>70%	Short practices in evenings or early morning

tice, and to drink 16 to 24 ounces of fluid for every pound lost. Fluids, such as water and sports drinks, are preferable during games and practices (suggested intakes are based on NATA [National Athletic Trainers' Association] recommendations).

- Replenish electrolytes, such as sodium (salt) and potassium, which are lost through sweat. The best way to replace these lost nutrients in addition to others such as carbohydrates (energy) and protien (muscle building) is by eating a balanced diet. Experts say that during the most intense training periods in the heat, additional salt intake may be helpful.

Cold

When a person is exposed to cold weather, body temperature starts to drop below normal. To counteract this, the body shivers to create heat and reduces blood flow to the extremities to conserve heat in the core of the body. But no matter how effective the body's natural heating mechanism is, the body will better withstand cold temperatures if it is prepared to handle them. To reduce the risk of cold-related illnesses, make sure players wear appropriate protective clothing and keep them active to maintain body heat. Also monitor the windchill because it can drastically affect the severity of players' responses to the weather. The windchill factor index is shown in table 4.2.

Table 4.2   Windchill Factor Index

Temperature (°F)

Wind speed (mph)	0	5	10	15	20	25	30	35	40
Flesh may freeze within one minute									
40	-55	-45	-35	-30	-20	-15	-5	0	10
35	-50	-40	-35	-30	-20	-10	-5	5	10
30	-50	-40	-30	-25	-20	-10	0	5	10
25	-45	-35	-30	-20	-15	-5	0	10	15
20	-35	-30	-25	-15	-10	0	5	10	20
15	-30	-25	-20	-10	-5	0	10	15	25
10	-20	-15	-10	0	5	10	15	20	30
5	-5	0	5	10	15	20	25	30	35

Windchill temperature (°F)

Severe Weather

Severe weather refers to a host of potential dangers, including lightning storms, tornadoes, hail, and heavy rains, which can cause injuries by creating sloppy field conditions. Lightning is of special concern because it can come up quickly and can cause great harm or even kill. For each 5-second count from the flash of lightning to the bang of thunder, lightning is one mile away. A flash-bang of 10 seconds means lightning is two miles away; a flash-bang of

15 seconds indicates lightning is three miles away. A practice or competition should be stopped for the day if lightning is three miles away or closer (15 seconds or less from flash to bang). In addition to these suggestions, your school, league, or state association may also have additional rules that you will want to consider in severe weather.

Safe places in which to take cover when lightning strikes are fully enclosed metal vehicles with the windows up, enclosed buildings, and low ground (under cover of bushes, if possible). It's not safe to be near metal objects such as flag poles, fences, light poles, and metal bleachers. Also avoid trees, water, and open fields.

Cancel practice when under either a tornado watch or warning. If you are practicing or competing when a tornado is nearby, you should get inside a building if possible. If you cannot get into a building, lie in a ditch or other low-lying area or crouch near a strong building and use your arms to protect your head and neck.

The keys to handling severe weather are caution and prudence. Don't try to get that last 10 minutes of practice in if lightning is on the horizon. Don't continue to play in heavy rain. Many storms can strike both quickly and ferociously. Respect the weather and play it safe.

Air Pollution

Poor air quality and smog can present real dangers to your players. Both short- and long-term lung damage are possible from participating in unsafe air. Although it's true that participating in clean air is not possible in many areas, restricting activity is recommended when the air-quality ratings are lower than moderate or when there is a smog alert. Your local health department or air-quality control board can inform you of the air-quality ratings for your area and when restricting activities is recommended.

Responding to Players' Injuries

No matter how good and thorough your prevention program is, injuries most likely will occur. When injury does strike, chances are you will be the one in charge. The severity and nature of the injury will determine how actively involved you'll be in treating it. But regardless of how seriously a player is hurt, it is your responsibility to know what steps to take. Therefore, you must be prepared to take appropriate action and provide basic emergency care when an injury occurs.

Being Prepared

Being prepared to provide basic emergency care involves many things, including being trained in cardiopulmonary resuscitation (CPR) and first aid and having an emergency plan.

CPR and First Aid Training

We recommend that all coaches receive CPR and first aid training from a nationally recognized organization such as the National Safety Council, the American Heart Association, the American Red Cross, or the American Sport Education Program (ASEP). You should be certified based on a practical test and a written test of knowledge. CPR training should include pediatric and adult basic life support and obstructed airway procedures.

First Aid Kit

A well-stocked first aid kit should include the following:

- Antibacterial soap or wipes
- Arm sling
- Athletic tape—one and a half inches
- Bandage scissors
- Bandage strips—assorted sizes
- Blood spill kit
- Cell phone
- Contact lens case
- Cotton swabs
- Elastic wraps—three inches, four inches, and six inches
- Emergency blanket
- Examination gloves—latex free
- Eye patch
- Face mask removal tool
- Foam rubber—one-eighth inch, one-fourth inch, and one-half inch
- Insect sting kit
- List of emergency phone numbers
- Mirror
- Moleskin

- Nail clippers
- Oral thermometer (to determine if an athlete has a fever caused by illness)
- Penlight
- Petroleum jelly
- Plastic bags for crushed ice
- Prewrap (underwrap for tape)
- Rescue breathing or CPR face mask
- Safety glasses (for first aiders)
- Safety pins
- Saline solution for eyes
- Sterile gauze pads—three-inch and four-inch squares (preferably nonstick)
- Sterile gauze rolls
- Sunscreen—sun protection factor (SPF) 30 or greater
- Tape adherent and tape remover
- Tongue depressors
- Tooth saver kit
- Triangular bandages
- Tweezers

Adapted, by permission, from M. Flegel, 2004, *Sport first aid,* 3rd ed. (Champaign, IL: Human Kinetics), 20.

Emergency Plan

An emergency plan is the final step in being prepared to take appropriate action for severe or serious injuries. The plan calls for three steps:

1. *Evaluate the injured player.*

   Use your CPR and first aid training to guide you. Be sure to keep these certifications up to date. Practice your skill frequently to keep them fresh and ready to use when you need them.

2. *Call the appropriate medical personnel.*

   If possible, delegate the responsibility for seeking medical help to another calm and responsible adult who attends all practices and games. Write out a list of emergency phone numbers and keep it with you at practices and games. Include the following phone numbers:

   - Rescue unit
   - Hospital
   - Physician
   - Police
   - Fire department

   Take each athlete's emergency information to every practice and game (see "Emergency Information Card" in appendix A on page 172). This information includes the person to contact in case of an emergency, what types of medications the athlete is using, what types of drugs the athlete is allergic to, and so on.

   Give an emergency response card (see "Emergency Response Card" in appendix A on page 173) to the contact person calling for emergency assistance. Having this information ready should help the contact person remain calm. You also must complete an injury report form and keep it on file for all injuries.

3. *Provide first aid.*

   If medical personnel are not on hand at the time of the injury, you should provide first aid care to the extent of your qualifications. Although your CPR and first aid training will guide you, it is important to remember the following:

   - Do not move the injured athlete if the injury is to the head, neck, or back; if a large joint (ankle, knee, elbow, shoulder) is dislocated; or if the pelvis, a rib, or an arm or leg is fractured.
   - Calm the injured athlete and keep others away from him as much as possible.
   - Evaluate whether the athlete's breathing has stopped or is irregular, and if necessary, clear the airway with your fingers.
   - Administer artificial respiration if the athlete's breathing has stopped. Administer CPR if the athlete's circulation has stopped.
   - Remain with the athlete until medical personnel arrive.

Emergency Steps

It is important that you have a clear, well-rehearsed emergency action plan. You want to be sure you are prepared in case of an emergency because every second counts.

Your emergency plan should follow this sequence:

1. Check the athlete's level of consciousness.
2. Send a contact person to call the appropriate medical personnel and to call the athlete's parents.
3. Send someone to wait for the rescue team and direct them to the injured athlete.
4. Assess the injury.
5. Administer first aid.
6. Assist emergency medical personnel in preparing the athlete for transportation to a medical facility.
7. Appoint someone to go with the athlete if the parents are not available. This person should be responsible, calm, and familiar with the athlete. Assistant coaches or parents are best for this job.
8. Complete an injury report form while the incident is fresh in your mind (see page 171 in appendix A).

Taking Appropriate Action

Proper CPR and first aid training, a well-stocked first aid kit, and an emergency plan help prepare you to take appropriate action when an injury occurs. We spoke in the previous section about the importance of providing first aid to the extent of your qualifications. Don't attempt to "play doctor" with injuries; sort out minor injuries that you can treat from those that need medical attention. Let's take a look at taking the appropriate action for minor injuries and more serious injuries.

Minor Injuries

Although no injury seems minor to the person experiencing it, most injuries are neither life threatening nor severe enough to restrict participation. When these injuries occur, you can take an active role in their initial treatment.

Scrapes and Cuts   When one of your players has an open wound, the first thing you should do is put on a pair of disposable latex-free examination gloves or some other effective blood barrier. Then follow these four steps:

1. Stop the bleeding by applying direct pressure with a clean dressing to the wound and elevating it. The player may be able to apply this pressure while you put on your gloves. Do not remove the dressing if it becomes soaked with blood. Instead, place an additional dressing on

Coaching Tip
You shouldn't let a fear of acquired immune deficiency syndrome (AIDS) and other communicable diseases stop you from helping a player. You are only at risk if you allow contaminated blood to come in contact with an open wound on your body, so the disposable examination gloves that you wear will protect you from AIDS should one of your players carry this disease. Check with your sport director, your sport league organization, or the Centers for Disease Control and Prevention (CDC) for more information about protecting yourself and your participants from AIDS.

top of the one already in place. If bleeding continues, elevate the injured area above the heart and maintain pressure.

2. Cleanse the wound thoroughly once the bleeding is controlled. A good rinsing with a forceful stream of water, and perhaps light scrubbing with soap, will help prevent infection.

3. Protect the wound with sterile gauze or a bandage strip. If the player continues to participate, apply protective padding over the injured area.

4. Remove and dispose of gloves carefully to prevent you or anyone else from coming into contact with blood.

For bloody noses not associated with serious facial injury, have the athlete sit and lean slightly forward. Then pinch the player's nostrils shut. If the bleeding continues after several minutes, or if the athlete has a history of nosebleeds, seek medical assistance.

Strains and Sprains   The physical demands of football practices and games often result in injury to the muscles or tendons (strains) or to the ligaments (sprains). When your players suffer minor strains or sprains, immediately apply the PRICE method of injury care:

P   Protect the athlete and injured body part from further danger or trauma.

R   Rest the area to avoid further damage and foster healing.

I   Ice the area to reduce swelling and pain.

C   Compress the area by securing an ice bag in place with an elastic wrap.

E   Elevate the injury above heart level to keep the blood from pooling in the area.

Bumps and Bruises   Inevitably, football players make contact with each other and with the ground. If the force applied to a body part at impact is great enough, a bump or bruise will result. Many players continue playing with these sore spots, but if the bump or bruise is large and painful, you should act appropriately. Again, use the PRICE method for injury care and monitor the injury. If swelling, discoloration, and pain have lessened, the player may resume participation with protective padding; if not, the player should be examined by a physician.

Serious Injuries

Head, neck, and back injuries; fractures; and injuries that cause a player to lose consciousness are among a class of injuries that you cannot and should not try to treat yourself. In these cases you should follow the emergency plan outlined on page 42. We do want to examine more closely, however, your role in preventing and handling heat exhaustion and heatstroke. Additionally, please refer to figure 4.1 for signs and symptoms associated with heat exhaustion and heatstroke.

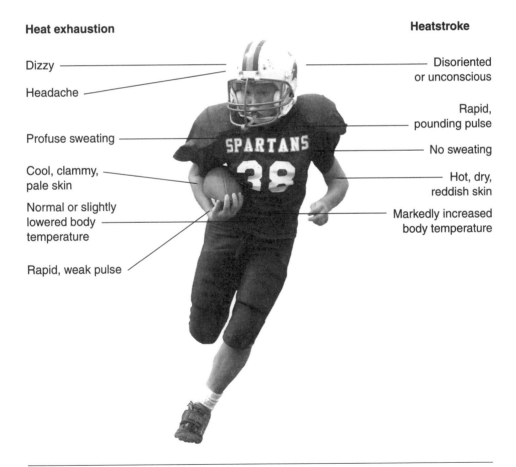

Heat exhaustion

Dizzy

Headache

Profuse sweating

Cool, clammy, pale skin

Normal or slightly lowered body temperature

Rapid, weak pulse

Heatstroke

Disoriented or unconscious

Rapid, pounding pulse

No sweating

Hot, dry, reddish skin

Markedly increased body temperature

Figure 4.1   Signs and symptoms of heat exhaustion and heatstroke.

Heat Cramps   Tough practices combined with heat stress and substantial fluid loss from sweating can provoke muscle cramps commonly known as heat cramps. Cramping is most common during the early part of the season when weather is the hottest and players may be least adapted to heat. The cramp, a severe tightening up of the muscle, can drop athletes and prevent continued play. Dehydration, electrolyte loss, and fatigue are the contributing factors. The immediate treatment is to have athletes cool off and slowly stretch the contracted muscle. Fluids with electrolytes should also be consumed to rehydrate the athlete. Athletes may return to play later that day or the next day provided the cramp doesn't cause a muscle strain.

Heat Exhaustion   Heat exhaustion is a shocklike condition caused by dehydration and electrolyte depletion. Symptoms include headache, nausea, dizziness, chills, fatigue, and extreme thirst. Profuse sweating is a key sign of heat exhaustion. Other signs include pale, cool, and clammy skin; rapid, weak pulse; loss of coordination; and dilated pupils.

A player suffering from heat exhaustion should rest in a cool, shaded area; drink cool fluids, particularly those containing electrolytes; and apply ice to the neck, back, or abdomen to help cool the body. If you believe a player is suffering from heat exhaustion, seek medical attention. Under no conditions should the athlete return to activity that day or before regaining all the weight lost through sweat. If the player has to see a physician, he shouldn't return to the team until he has a written release from the physician.

Heatstroke   Heatstroke is a life-threatening condition in which the body stops sweating and body temperature rises dangerously high. It occurs when dehydration causes a malfunction in the body's temperature control center in the brain. Symptoms include the feeling of being extremely hot, nausea, confusion, irritability, and fatigue. Signs include hot, dry, and flushed or red skin (this is a key sign); lack of sweat; rapid pulse; rapid breathing; constricted pupils; vomiting; diarrhea; and possibly seizures, unconsciousness, or respiratory or cardiac arrest.

If a player experiences heatstroke, send for emergency medical assistance immediately and cool the player as quickly as possible. Remove excess clothing and equipment from the player, and cool his body with cool, wet towels or by pouring cool water over him or place him in a cold water bath. Apply ice packs to the armpits, neck, back, abdomen, and between the legs. If the player is conscious, give him cool fluids to drink. If the player is unconscious, place him on his side to allow fluids and vomit to drain from the mouth. An athlete who has suffered heatstroke may not return to the team until getting a written release from a physician.

Protecting Yourself

When one of your players is injured, naturally your first concern is the player's well-being. Your feelings for youngsters, after all, are what made you decide to coach. Unfortunately, you must consider something else: Can you be held liable for the injury?

From a legal standpoint, a coach must fulfill nine duties. We've discussed all but planning in this chapter (planning is discussed in chapters 5 and 10). The following is a summary of your legal duties:

1. Provide a safe environment.
2. Properly plan the activity.
3. Provide adequate and proper equipment.
4. Match athletes.
5. Warn of inherent risks in the sport.
6. Supervise the activity closely.
7. Evaluate athletes for injury or incapacitation.
8. Know emergency procedures, CPR, and first aid.
9. Keep adequate records.

In addition to fulfilling these nine legal duties, you should check your organization's insurance coverage and your insurance coverage to make sure these policies will properly protect you from liability.

5

Teaching and Shaping Skills

Coaching football is about teaching kids how to play the game by teaching them technique, fitness, and values. It's also about "coaching" players before, during, and after contests. Teaching and coaching are closely related, but there are important differences. In this chapter we focus on the principles of teaching, especially on teaching technical skills and tactics. But these principles apply to teaching fitness concepts and values as well. Armed with these principles, you will be able to design effective and efficient practices and will understand how to deal with misbehavior. Then you will be able to teach the skills and plays necessary to be successful in football that are outlined in chapters 6, 7, and 8.

Teaching Football Skills

Many people believe that the only qualification needed to teach a skill is to have performed it. Although it's helpful to have performed it, teaching it successfully requires much more than that. And even if you haven't performed the skill before, you can learn to teach successfully with the useful acronym IDEA:

I   Introduce the skill.

D   Demonstrate the skill.

E   Explain the skill.

A   Attend to players practicing the skill.

Introduce the Skill

Players, especially those who are young and inexperienced, need to know which skill they are learning and why they are learning it. You should therefore follow these three steps every time you introduce a skill to your players:

1. Get your players' attention.
2. Name the skill.
3. Explain the importance of the skill.

Get Your Players' Attention

Because youngsters are easily distracted, do something to get their attention. Some coaches use interesting news items or stories. Others use jokes. And still others simply project enthusiasm to get their players to listen. Whatever method you use, speak slightly above your normal volume and look your players in the eye when you speak.

Also, position players so that they can see and hear you. Arrange the players in two or three evenly spaced rows, facing you. (Make sure they aren't looking into the sun or at a distracting activity.) Then ask if all of them can see you before you begin to speak.

Name the Skill

Although there may be other common names for the skill you are introducing, decide as a staff before the start of the season which one you'll use and stick with it. This will help prevent confusion and enhance communication among your players. When you introduce the new skill, name it so that the players automatically correlate the name with the skill in later discussions.

Explain the Importance of the Skill

As Rainer Martens, the founder of the American Sport Education Program (ASEP), has said, "The most difficult aspect of coaching is this: Coaches must learn to let athletes learn. Sport skills should be taught so they have meaning to the child, not just meaning to the coach." Although the importance of a skill may be apparent to you, your players may be less able to see how the skill will help them become better football players. Offer them a reason for learning the skill and describe how the skill relates to more advanced skills.

Demonstrate the Skill

The demonstration step is the most important part of teaching sport skills to players who may never have done anything closely resembling it. They need a picture, not just words. They need to see how the skill is performed. If you are unable to perform the skill correctly, ask an assistant coach, one of your players, or someone more skilled to perform the demonstration.

These tips will help make your demonstrations more effective:

- Use correct form.
- Demonstrate the skill several times.
- Slow the action, if possible, during one or two performances so players can see every movement involved in the skill.
- Perform the skill at different angles so your players can get a full perspective of it.
- Demonstrate the skill with both the right and the left arms or legs.

Explain the Skill

Players learn more effectively when they're given a brief explanation of the skill along with the demonstration. Use simple terms and, if possible, relate the skill to previously learned skills. Ask your players whether they understand your description. A good technique is to ask the team to repeat your explanation. Ask questions like "What are you going to do first?" and "Then what?" Should players look confused or uncertain, repeat your explanation and demonstration. If possible, use different words so that your players get a chance to try to understand the skill from a different perspective.

Complex skills often are better understood when they are explained in more manageable parts. For instance, if you want to teach your players how to provide pass protection blocking, you might take the following steps:

1. Show them a correct performance of the entire skill and explain its function in football.
2. Break down the skill and point out its component parts to your players.
3. Have players perform each of the component skills you have already taught them, such as proper body position, delivering a blow to stop the defensive charge, and proper footwork.
4. After players have demonstrated their ability to perform the separate parts of the skill in sequence, reexplain the entire skill.
5. Have players practice the skill in gamelike conditions.

Young players have short attention spans. Long demonstration or explanation of a skill may cause them to lose focus. Therefore, spend no more than a few minutes altogether on the introduction, demonstration, and explanation phases. Then involve the players in drills or games that call on them to perform the skill.

Attend to Players Practicing the Skill

If the skill you selected was within your players' capabilities and you have done an effective job of introducing, demonstrating, and explaining it, your players should be ready to attempt the skill. Some players may need to be physically guided through the movements during their first few attempts. Walking unsure athletes through the skill this way will help them gain the confidence to perform the skill on their own.

Look at the entire technique, and then break it down into components. For example, when teaching a defensive back to cover man to man, your drill sequence could consist of the following:

1. Stance
2. Start
3. Backpedal
4. Angle backpedal
5. Leaving the backpedal
6. Pattern recognition and pattern reaction

Each segment of the drill should take only a minute or two once the players master the skill, and it will provide them with the needed tools to play man-to-man coverage.

How to Properly Run Your Drills

Before running a drill that teaches technique, you should do the following:

- Name the drill.
- Explain the skill or skills to be taught.
- Position the players correctly.
- Explain what the drill will accomplish.
- State the command that will start the drill, such as a snap count or "Hut."
- State the command that will end the drill, such as a whistle.

Once the drill has been introduced and repeated a few times in this manner, you will find that merely calling out the name of the drill is sufficient, and your players will automatically line up in the proper position to run the drill and practice the skill.

Your teaching duties, though, don't end when all your athletes have demonstrated that they understand how to perform a skill. In fact, your teaching role is just beginning as you help your players improve their skills. A significant part of your teaching consists of closely observing the hit-and-miss trial performances of your players. You will shape players' skills by detecting errors and correcting them using positive feedback. Keep in mind that your positive feedback will have a great influence on your players' motivation to practice and improve their performances.

Remember, too, that players may need individual instruction. So set aside a time before, during, or after practice to give individual help.

Helping Players Improve Skills

After you have successfully taught your players the fundamentals of a skill, your focus will be on helping them improve it. Players learn skills and improve upon them at different rates, so don't get frustrated if progress seems slow. Instead, help players improve by shaping their skills and detecting and correcting errors.

Shaping Players' Skills

One of your principal teaching duties is to reward positive effort and behavior—in terms of successful skill execution—when you see it. A defensive lineman neutralizes, defeats, and sheds a blocker and moves to get in on the tackle, and you immediately say, "That's the way to do it! Great effort and pursuit!" This, plus a smile and a thumbs-up gesture, go a long way toward reinforcing that technique in that player. However, sometimes you may have a long, dry spell before you see correct techniques to reinforce. It's difficult to reward players when they don't execute skills correctly. How can you shape their skills if this is the case?

Shaping skills takes practice on your players' part and patience on yours. Expect your players to make errors. Telling the player who made the tackle that he did a good job doesn't ensure that he'll have the same success next time. Seeing inconsistency in your players' technique can be frustrating. It's even more challenging to stay positive when your athletes repeatedly perform a skill incorrectly or lack enthusiasm for learning. It can certainly be frustrating to see athletes who seemingly don't heed your advice and continue to make the same mistakes. And when the athletes don't seem to care, you may wonder why you should.

Please know that it is normal to get frustrated sometimes when teaching skills. Nevertheless, part of successful coaching is controlling this frustration. Instead of getting upset, use these six guidelines for shaping skills:

1. *Think small initially.*

   Reward the first signs of behavior that approximate what you want. Then reward closer and closer approximations of the desired behavior. In short, use your reward power to shape the behavior you seek.

2. *Break skills into small steps.*

   For instance, in learning to execute a pass protect block, one of your players does well in the initial move and setup but stands up too straight and doesn't get into good hitting position, making it easier for defenders to move around him. Reinforce the correct technique in the initial move and setup, and then teach the player how to get into the correct hitting position by keeping the head up and rear end down. Once he masters this, shift the focus to getting him to keep his feet shoulder-width apart.

3. *Develop one component of a skill at a time.*

   Don't try to shape two components of a skill at once. For example, in dropping back to throw a pass, quarterbacks must first secure the snap from the center and then use one of the drop steps—the crossover, the backpedal, or the rollout. Players should focus first on one aspect (receiving the snap from the center, using good hand positioning, and presenting a good target for the center), then on the other (dropping back and using one of the techniques just mentioned). Athletes who have problems mastering a skill often do so because they're trying to improve two or more components at once. Help these athletes to isolate a single component.

4. *As athletes become more proficient at a skill, reinforce them only occasionally and only for the best examples of the skill behavior.*

   By focusing only on the best examples of a skill, you will help players continue to improve once they've mastered the basics.

5. *When athletes are trying to master a new skill, temporarily relax your standards for how you reward them.*

   As players focus on the new skill or attempt to integrate it with other skills, the old, well-learned skills may temporarily degenerate.

6. *Go back to the basics.*

   If, however, a well-learned skill degenerates for long, you may need to restore it by going back to the basics.

Coaches often have more-skilled players provide feedback to teammates as they practice skills. This can be effective, but proceed with caution: You must tell the skilled players exactly what to look for when their teammates are performing the skills. You must also tell them the corrections for the common errors of that skill.

Detecting and Correcting Errors

Good coaches recognize that athletes make two types of errors: learning errors and performance errors. Learning errors are those that occur because athletes don't know how to perform a skill; that is, they have not yet developed the correct motor pattern in the brain to perform a particular skill. Performance errors are made not because athletes don't know how to execute the skill, but because they have made a mistake in executing what they do know. There is no easy way to know whether a player is making learning or performance errors, and part of the art of coaching is being able to sort out which type of error each mistake is.

The process of helping your athletes correct errors begins with your observing and evaluating their performances to determine if the mistakes are learning or performance errors. Carefully watch your athletes to see if they routinely make the errors in both practice and game settings, or if the errors tend to occur only in game settings. If the latter is the case, then your athletes are making performance errors. For performance errors, you need to look for the reasons your athletes are not performing as well as they know how; perhaps they are nervous, or maybe they get distracted by the game setting. Find out the reason for the decline in performance and help them to tackle those issues. If the mistakes are learning errors, then you need to help them learn the skill, which is the focus of this section.

When correcting learning errors, there is no substitute for the coach knowing the skills well. The better you understand a skill—not only how it is performed correctly but also what causes learning errors—the more helpful you will be in correcting mistakes.

One of the most common coaching mistakes is to provide inaccurate feedback and advice on how to correct errors. Don't rush into error correction; wrong feedback or poor advice will hurt the learning process more than no feedback or advice at all. If you are uncertain about the cause of the problem or how to correct it, continue to observe and analyze until you are more sure. As a rule, you should see the error repeated several times before attempting to correct it.

Correct One Error at a Time

Suppose Danny, one of your wide receivers, is having trouble catching deep passes over his shoulder. He's getting open, but you notice that he's not reaching back with both hands so that he sees both the ball and his hands at the moment of the catch. You also notice that his hands are not positioned correctly when he catches the ball. What do you do?

First, decide which error to correct first, because athletes learn more effectively when they attempt to correct one error at a time. Determine whether one error is causing the other; if so, have the athlete correct that error first, because it may eliminate the other error. In Danny's case, however, neither error is causing the other, but they are related. In such cases, athletes should correct the error that is the easiest to correct and will bring the greatest improvement when remedied. For Danny, this probably means placing his little fingers together to receive the ball and then working on reaching back with both hands to make the catch. Improvement in his hand position will likely motivate him to correct the error of not reaching back to see his hands and the ball at the moment of the catch.

Coaching Tip
Eliminate starting your feedback to players with the word "Don't." By telling them what you want them to do instead of what not to do, you will create success rather than failure.

Use Positive Feedback to Correct Errors

The positive approach to correcting errors includes emphasizing what to do instead of what not to do. Use compliments, praise, rewards, and encouragement to correct errors. Acknowledge correct performance as well as efforts to improve. By using positive feedback, you can help your athletes feel good about themselves and promote a strong desire to achieve.

When you're working with one athlete at a time, the positive approach to correcting errors includes four steps:

1. *Praise effort and correct performance.*

   Praise your athlete for trying to perform a skill correctly and for performing any parts of it correctly. Praise the athlete immediately after he performs the skill, if possible. Keep the praise simple: "Good try," "Way to hustle," "Good form," or "That's the way to follow through." You can also use nonverbal feedback, such as smiling, clapping your hands, or any facial or body expression that shows approval.

Make sure you're sincere with your praise. Don't indicate that an athlete's effort was good when it wasn't. Usually an athlete knows when he has made a sincere effort to perform the skill correctly and perceives undeserved praise for what it is—untruthful feedback to make him feel good. Likewise, don't indicate that a player's performance was correct when it wasn't.

2. *Give simple and precise feedback to correct errors.*

Don't burden a player with a long or detailed explanation of how to correct an error. Give just enough feedback that the player can correct one error at a time. Before giving feedback, recognize that some athletes readily accept it immediately after the error; others will respond better if you slightly delay the correction.

For errors that are complicated to explain and difficult to correct, try the following:

- Explain and demonstrate what the athlete should have done. Do not demonstrate what the athlete did wrong.

- Explain the cause or causes of the error, if it isn't obvious.

- Explain why you are recommending the correction you have selected, if it's not obvious.

3. *Make sure the athlete understands your feedback.*

If the athlete doesn't understand your feedback, he won't be able to correct the error. Ask the athlete to repeat the feedback and to explain and demonstrate how it will be used. If he can't do this, be patient and present your feedback again. Then ask the athlete to repeat the feedback after you're finished.

4. *Provide an environment that motivates the athlete to improve.*

Your players won't always be able to correct their errors immediately, even if they do understand your feedback. Encourage them to "hang tough" and stick with it when corrections are difficult or they seem discouraged. For more difficult corrections, remind them that it will take time, and the improvement will happen only if they work at it. Encourage players with little self-confidence. Saying something like, "You were catching the football much better today; with practice, you'll be able to watch the ball into your hands and catch all of them," can motivate a player to continue to refine his receiving skills.

Other players may be very self-motivated and need little help from you in this area; with them you can practically ignore step 4 when correcting an error. Although motivation comes from within, try to provide an environment of positive instruction and encouragement to help your athletes improve.

A final note on correcting errors: Team sports such as football provide unique challenges in this endeavor. How do you provide individual feedback in a group setting using a positive approach? Instead of yelling across the field to correct an error (and embarrass the player), substitute for the player who erred, and then make the correction on the sidelines. This type of feedback has three advantages:

- The player will be more receptive to the one-on-one feedback.

- The other players are still active and still practicing skills and unable to hear your discussion.

- Because the rest of the team is still playing, you'll feel compelled to make your comments simple and concise—which is more helpful to the player.

This doesn't mean you can't use the team setting to give specific, positive feedback. You can do so to emphasize correct group and individual performances. Use this team-feedback approach only for positive statements, though. Keep negative feedback for individual discussions.

> **Coaching Tip**
> Recognize that the introduction of competition and contact may initially adversely affect an athlete's focus on learning proper skills, but with practice this can be overcome. Start your teaching at half speed and then as the skill is mastered and the players become comfortable executing the skill, you can increase the level of contact and competition.

Dealing With Misbehavior

Athletes will misbehave at times; it's only natural. You can respond to misbehavior in two ways: extinction or discipline.

Extinction

Ignoring a misbehavior—neither rewarding nor disciplining it—is called extinction. This can be effective in certain circumstances. In some situations, disciplining young people's misbehavior only encourages them to act up further because of the recognition they get. Ignoring misbehavior teaches youngsters that it is not worth your attention.

Sometimes, though, you cannot wait for a behavior to fizzle out. When players cause danger to themselves or others or disrupt the activities of others, you need to take immediate action. Tell the offending player that the behavior must stop and that discipline will follow if it doesn't. If the athlete doesn't stop misbehaving after the warning, use discipline.

Extinction also doesn't work well when a misbehavior is self-rewarding. For example, you may be able to keep from grimacing if a youngster kicks you in the shin, but even so, he still knows you were hurt. Therein lies the reward. In these circumstances, it is also necessary to discipline the player for the undesirable behavior.

Extinction works best in situations in which players are seeking recognition through mischievous behaviors, clowning, or grandstanding. Usually, if you are patient, their failure to get your attention will cause the behavior to disappear.

However, be sure that you don't extinguish desirable behavior. When youngsters do something well, they expect to be positively reinforced. Not rewarding them will likely cause them to discontinue the desired behavior.

Discipline

Some educators say we should never discipline young people, but should only reinforce their positive behaviors. They argue that discipline does not work, that it creates hostility and sometimes develops avoidance behaviors that may be more unwholesome than the original problem behavior. It is true that discipline does not always work and that it can create problems when used ineffectively, but when used appropriately, discipline is effective in eliminating undesirable behaviors without creating other undesirable consequences. You must use discipline effectively, because it is impossible to guide athletes through positive reinforcement and extinction alone. Discipline is part of the positive approach when these guidelines are followed:

- Discipline in a corrective way to help athletes improve now and in the future. Don't discipline to retaliate and make yourself feel better.
- Impose discipline in an impersonal way when athletes break team rules or otherwise misbehave. Shouting at or scolding athletes indicates that your attitude is one of revenge.
- Once a rule has been agreed upon, ensure that athletes who violate it experience the unpleasant consequences of their misbehavior. Don't wave discipline threateningly over their heads. Just do it, but warn an athlete once before disciplining.
- Be consistent in administering discipline.
- Don't discipline using consequences that may cause you guilt. If you can't think of an appropriate consequence right away, tell the player you will talk with him after you think about it. You might consider involving the player in designing a consequence.
- Once the discipline is completed, don't make athletes feel that they are "in the doghouse." Always make them feel that they're valued members of the team.
- Make sure that what you think is discipline isn't perceived by the athlete as a positive reinforcement, for instance, keeping a player out of doing

a certain drill or portion of the practice may be just what the athlete desired.

- Never discipline athletes for making errors when they are playing.
- Never use physical activity—running laps or doing push-ups—as discipline. To do so only causes athletes to resent physical activity, something we want them to learn to enjoy throughout their lives.
- Discipline sparingly. Constant discipline and criticism cause athletes to turn their interests elsewhere and to resent you as well.

6

Coaching Offense

This chapter focuses on the offensive techniques and tactics your players need to perform effectively in youth football games. Remember to use the IDEA approach to teaching skills: introduce, demonstrate, and explain the skill, and attend to players as they practice the skill (see page 50 in chapter 5). This chapter also ties directly to the season plans in chapter 10, describing the technical skills and the team tactics that you'll teach at the practices outlined there. If you aren't familiar with football skills, rent or purchase a video so you can see the skills performed correctly. Also, the *Coaching Youth Football Online Course* offered by the American Sport Education Program (ASEP) and USA Football can help you further understand these skills. (You can take this course by going to www.asep.com/coachingyouthfootball.)

Because the information in this book is limited to football basics, you will need to advance your knowledge as a coach as your players advance in their skills. You can do this by learning from your experiences, watching and talking with more experienced coaches, and studying resources on advanced skills.

Offensive Technical Skills

The offensive technical skills you will teach your players are assuming a proper stance, blocking, running the ball, playing quarterback, receiving, and centering the ball. Mastering these techniques will allow your offensive players to better execute your offensive tactics—or plays—during the game. These basic skills serve as the foundation for playing football well at all levels. Football players practice these techniques at every practice from youth football to the pros.

Stance

The stance is the proper alignment of a player's body at the start of each play. Following is a description of the stances you should teach players at each offensive position.

Coaching Tip

Beginners may feel uncomfortable in this stance and may adjust their feet so that one foot is way behind the other. When you see this, ask them to bring the back foot forward so that it is no more offset than toe to instep. A more even foot alignment allows them to step easily with either foot.

Offensive Line

When teaching your offensive linemen their stance, start with a four-point stance, as shown in figure 6.1, then move to a three-point stance as needed. To assume a four-point stance, coach the linemen to do the following:

- Stand with feet shoulder-width apart with weight balanced evenly on both feet and toes aligned.
- Bend the knees and rest a forearm on the inside of each thigh.

- Reach straight out with both hands slightly in front of the shoulders.
- Keep the back straight, head up, and shoulders even.

This stance is used for straight-ahead blocking or blocking to one side or the other. It forms a good foundation for adjustments to a three-point stance.

Once offensive linemen are comfortable with a four-point stance, instruct them to lift one hand and adjust the position of the feet slightly into a three-point stance (see figure 6.2). Use these points to teach the offensive linemen to assume a three-point stance:

Figure 6.1   Proper four-point stance for offensive linemen.

- Place the feet shoulder-width apart, in a heel–instep relationship, with the dominant foot back.
- Put very little weight on the down hand to allow for quick forward, backward, and lateral movement.
- Place the left arm loosely across the left thigh.
- Keep the back straight, with the head up to see defenders across the line of scrimmage. This position is the strongest and safest for the back and neck.

Check to see that player's shoulders and back are level. If the shoulders are cocked, the down hand is usually in the center of the blocker's body and needs to be moved more to the outside of the blocker's shoulder. When the back is angled, the blocker needs to bring the rear end up and decrease the angle of flex in the legs.

Figure 6.2   Proper three-point stance for offensive linemen.

Figure 6.3   Proper two-point stance for receivers.

Coaching Tip

Check to make sure that receivers move forward on the snap and don't step back to start. They should roll over the front foot and step across the line of scrimmage with the back foot.

Receivers

Receivers use two basic types of stances. The first stance used by wide receivers is a two-point, or upright, stance (see figure 6.3). Its advantages are that receivers can get off the line of scrimmage without being held up and that they are in immediate position to receive quick passes. To assume a two-point stance, receivers should do the following:

- Place the feet shoulder-width apart, in a heel–toe relationship, with the foot closest to the football back slightly more than the other.
- Bend the knees in a comfortable position.
- Keep weight on the balls of the feet with a majority of weight on the front foot.
- Keep the back straight, leaning forward slightly.
- Square the shoulders to the line of scrimmage.
- Hold the arms in a comfortable position.
- Turn the head in to the center of the field so that the player can check his alignment and see the ball when it is snapped.

The second stance is a three-point stance, in which receivers distribute their weight evenly, with their heads up and eyes focused either directly downfield or on the football (see figure 6.4). The feet are staggered, which allows good explosion from the line of scrimmage. To assume the three-point stance, receivers should do the following:

- Place the feet shoulder-width apart, in a heel–toe relationship, with the foot closest to the football staggered in a comfortable sprinter's position.
- Point knees and toes straight ahead.
- Keep the back straight, parallel to the ground, and head up looking into the ball.

Make sure that receivers in a three-point stance drive forward and don't rise up as they come out of their stance to release from the line; check to see that the majority of their weight is on the down hand and front foot.

Figure 6.4 Proper three-point stance for receivers.

Center

To help young players get in proper position to make the snap to the quarterback, have centers assume a four-point stance and then lift up their snapping hand to place the ball on the ground where they can easily grasp it (see figure 6.5). Later, if they are in the position correctly, they can progress to a three-point stance with the nonsnapping hand and forearm resting on the thigh. To assume a four-point stance, centers should do the following:

Figure 6.5 Proper four-point stance for centers.

- Start in an upright stance.
- Position the feet shoulder-width apart with the toe of the foot on the side of the snapping hand even with the instep of the other foot.
- Bend at the knees until the forearms rest comfortably on the thighs.
- Reach straight out with both hands so that they are on the ground slightly in front of the shoulder pads.
- Lift the snapping hand and place the ball in position. The ball should be placed with the laces to the outside and rotated slightly toward the ground.
- Grasp the front half of the ball with the fingers over the laces and prepare to lift and turn the ball sideways so that the quarterback can take the snap.

Make certain that centers have their back straight and shoulders even before the snap. They should keep the ball even with the shoulder pad on the side of the snapping hand.

Quarterback

A quarterback's stance must be poised and relaxed, reflecting confidence. The quarterback's feet should be comfortably spread, approximately shoulder-width apart and as close to the center's feet as possible. Quarterbacks should bend their knees slightly and drop their hips while remaining as tall over the center as possible. It is the quarterbacks' responsibility to adjust the height of their stance to fit each center. Quarterbacks' shoulders should be parallel to the line of scrimmage, their heads up to check the position of the defense. See figure 6.6 for an example of a proper quarterback's stance.

Coaching Tip

Beginning quarterbacks often bend at the waist and position their feet too far from the center's feet. When you see this, move them closer to the center and instruct them to bend their knees so that they can reach under the center to take the snap.

Figure 6.6   Proper stance for quarterbacks.

Running Backs

The most common stance for halfbacks and fullbacks is a two-point stance (see figure 6.7). In this position running backs are in an upright stance with the head up, which allows them to see the quarterback and the offensive line. Players at these positions must accelerate quickly from their backfield spot. Before the ball is snapped, running backs should do the following:

- Stand with feet about shoulder-width apart and weight on the balls of the feet.
- Keep feet nearly parallel to allow a quick burst in any direction.
- Bend knees slightly and place hands on the knees.
- Keep the head up and eyes looking ahead.

Coaching Tip

Be sure that running backs move either forward or laterally on the snap, based on the play called in the huddle. If they step back to get started, adjust their weight on the down hand so that they can move easily in any direction. Stepping back usually occurs when running backs do not anticipate where they should move on the snap. Moving the hand back a few inches creates a balanced stance with the weight on the balls of both feet.

If your running backs use the four- or three-point stance, teach them the same technique for getting into their stance that you teach the offensive line players.

Figure 6.7   Proper two-point stance for running backs.

Blocking

Blocking is the cornerstone of all successful offensive teams. Teams use blocking to move a defensive player out of the area where they want to run the football and to keep defensive line players from tackling the quarterback.

Offensive line players block in some manner on every play. Running backs block when they are not carrying the football, and wide receivers block when they are not catching the football. You can start by teaching your football players basic blocks, blocks that are critical for a successful youth football program. Then, as your team becomes more experienced you may want to add more advanced blocks.

Basic Blocks

Basic blocks allow a diverse offensive attack and are the easiest for you to teach and your players to learn. Therefore, it is important that your team masters the basic blocks used in youth football. These include the drive block, the hook block, the angle block, and the cross block.

Drive Block   The drive block is a one-on-one block used most often when a defensive line player lined up directly over an offensive player must be moved for the play to succeed (see figure 6.8). When teaching your players the drive block, emphasize these points:

Figure 6.8   Drive block.

- Explode from the stance with the foot closest to the opponent and drive the hips forward on the third and fourth steps through the block.
- Start with short, choppy steps and keep the feet moving.
- Step with the foot on the side of the shoulder they are using to block.
- Deliver the block from a wide base and keep the head up and shoulders square.
- Anticipate the forward movement of the defensive player.
- Keep the head on the side of the opponent toward the hole and make first contact with the opposite shoulder pad.
- Come off low and get under the pads of the defensive linemen.

- As the pad makes contact, punch hands into the opponent to establish momentum and deliver the blow on impact with the hands or forearms, not the head.
- Follow through with short, choppy steps, turning the opponent away from the hole.

If blockers are pushed to one side and fall off their block, make sure that they have a wide base and have not narrowed the split between their feet as they make contact with the defensive player.

Coaching Tip

Offensive line blockers should drive the palm of the inside hand directly into the defensive player's chest as they take their second step. This will stop the forward movement of the defensive player and allow the offensive blocker to position the body to the outside.

Drive-Blocking Drill

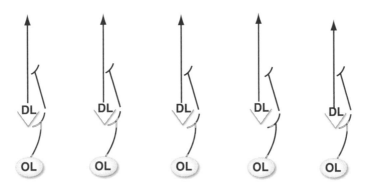

Offensive linemen (OL) act as blockers and line up directly in front of defensive linemen (DL) as shown in the diagram. The coach tells the OL which shoulder to use for the block. OL drive the DL straight back off the line using their left shoulders, arms, and hands. OL drive the DL behind the line for two or three steps until the whistle is blown. Repeat drill using the opposite shoulder.

Hook Block   Use the hook block when blocking a defensive player located on the blocker's outside shoulder and running the ball to the outside of the block. The blocker seals off the opposing end so that the running back can run around the end to the outside. The blocker takes a short lateral step with the outside foot (see figure 6.9a), makes contact with the second step (see figure 6.9b), and swings around to contain the rusher (see figure 6.9c). The blocker hits the defender at or slightly above waist level and keeps the point of contact to the side on which the sweep is being run. When teaching your players the hook block, emphasize these points:

- Remain low.
- Step laterally with the foot opposite the side of the shoulder used to block. The first lateral step should be short and quick.
- Come off low and get under the pads of the defensive lineman.
- Take the second step directly toward the center of the defensive player's chest, driving the palm of the hand directly into the chest of the defensive lineman. The other hand should drive up and under the shoulder pad of the defensive lineman.
- Position the body so the defensive player cannot move to the outside.

a

b

c

Figure 6.9   *(a-c)* Hook block.

Hook-Blocking Drill

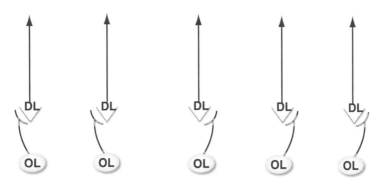

Offensive linemen (OL) act as blockers and line up on the inside shoulder of the defensive linemen (DL) as shown in the diagram. The coach tells the OL which shoulder to use for the block. The OL keep the DL from working to the outside by driving them back with their far shoulders, arms, and hands until the whistle is blown. Repeat drill using the opposite shoulder.

Angle Block   The angle block is used to block a defensive player located on the blocker's inside shoulder, the inside gap, or in front of the offensive lineman to the inside. The blocker takes a short directional step to the inside and in front of where the defensive player lined up as shown in figure 6.10. When teaching players the angle block, emphasize these points:

- Anticipate the defensive player's forward movement.
- Explode off of the outside foot (see figure 6.10a) and make contact with the outside shoulder pad into the side of the defensive player (see figure 6.10b).

a   b

Figure 6.10   *(a-b)* Angle block.

- Keep the head in front of the defensive man, cutting off penetration.
- Drive the defensive player down the line.

When blockers fail to get their heads in front, adjust the angle of the first step so that it is in front of the defensive player's alignment. This adjustment puts blockers in the proper position to stop the defensive player's movement across the line of scrimmage.

Angle-Blocking Drill

Offensive linemen (OL) act as blockers and line up in front of defensive linemen (DL) as shown in the diagram. The coach tells the OL which shoulder to use for the block. OL keep the DL from penetrating down the line by driving them back and blocking with the shoulder until the whistle is blown. OL should try to get their heads in front of the DL. Repeat drill using the opposite shoulder.

Cross Block   The cross block can be used to create an element of surprise, to adjust for a mismatch at the line of scrimmage, or to block against a defensive alignment that is difficult to block straight on. In this block, two adjacent players work together to block two defensive players. When both defensive players are on the line of scrimmage, the outside blocker will usually go first using an angle block. When one defensive player is on the line and the other is lined up off the line (in a linebacker position) (see figure 6.11a), the player blocking the defensive player on the line will go first. The second player on the cross block needs to take a short drop step with the foot on the side of the block (see figure 6.11b), allow the first blocker to move, and then staying low, drive into the assigned defensive player (see figure 6.11c). Blocking form and execution are the same except for the timing between the blockers. Cross blocks can be performed by teammates who line up next to each other—a center and guard, a guard and tackle, a tackle and tight end. This is a bang-bang play; timing and explosive power are the keys.

Coaching Tip

Have players practice blocking against air, handheld shields, or lightweight standup blocking bags to see just how fast they can execute the cross block. Speed in executing the block gives the offensive linemen the opportunity to move into their block before the defensive player has a chance to react.

Figure 6.11   *(a-c)* Cross block.

When you see the timing between the two blockers is off, make sure that the second blocker is not waiting on the first to get all the way into his block before starting to move to his defensive player. The second blocker should step back and then drive to his block at the same time the other player moves into his block.

Cross-Blocking Drill

Players divide into groups of four with two offensive linemen (OL) who act as blockers and two defensive linemen (DL) as shown in the diagram. The coach tells the OL which shoulder to use for the block. The outside OL blocks first, and as the first OL is blocking, the second OL steps back with his first step to provide room for the first blocker to clear. The OL should separate the two DL by opening a running lane. Both OL should use their shoulders to block and get their heads in front of the defensive player. The OL will drive until the whistle is blown. Repeat drill using the opposite shoulder.

Advanced Blocks

Once your team has mastered the basic blocks, you can begin to teach them more advanced blocking skills. Advanced blocks require a great deal of coordination, and the two offensive blockers must work as one unit. This coordination takes time to practice and should be introduced after the basic blocks have been mastered. The advanced blocks include the double-team block, the zone block, the downfield block, and the pass protection block.

Double-Team Block   The double-team block should be used when you need two adjacent blockers working together on one defensive player. When the blockers execute the block correctly, it becomes one of the offense's most powerful blocks. The blockers move simultaneously: the inside blocker using a drive block and the outside blocker using an angle block.

The blockers should drive the defensive player down and off the line of scrimmage. The inside blocker should step with the outside foot directly at the midsection of the defensive player and hit with the outside shoulder pad. The outside blocker should step down with the inside foot and, on the second step, drive the outside shoulder pad into the side of the defensive player.

When contact is made, both blockers should bring their hips together (inside blocker's outside hip to outside blocker's inside hip) to provide a combined push against the defensive player. See figure 6.12 for an example of the double-team block.

Coaching Tip

If the defensive player is able to split the two blockers, make certain that the blockers bring their hips together as they work to drive the defensive player off the line.

Figure 6.12   Double-team block.

Double Team—Blocking Drill

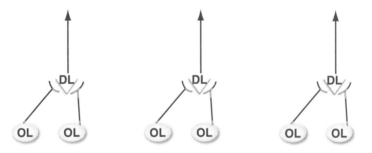

Players divide into groups of three with two offensive linemen (OL) who act as blockers and one defensive lineman (DL) as shown in the diagram. The inside OL uses the outside shoulder, and the outside OL uses the inside shoulder to make the block so that they can come together and generate as much power as possible against the DL. The OL drive until the whistle is blown. Repeat the drill using the opposite shoulders.

Zone Block   The zone block is a combination block using two offensive players against two defensive players. It is most often used against a defensive lineman and a linebacker who may or may not be stunting. The zone block is very difficult to teach and should be added to your team's blocking scheme only after the previous blocks have been mastered. This blocking scheme requires that the two blockers read the defensive player's movement together. It is usually used against a defense where the outside blocker has a defensive lineman lined up in front of him and the adjacent inside blocker has a linebacker lined up in front of him.

Coaching Tip

When the defensive lineman penetrates across the line, go back and make certain that the two blockers are giving first priority to blocking this player before either one moves off to pick up the linebacker.

With the ball being run to the outside, on the snap, both blockers move together. Both players should step laterally with the outside foot. The outside player should use a hook block technique and stop the charge of the defensive player with the second step. The inside player should see the linebacker and determine if he is moving to the outside behind the defensive lineman or charging straight ahead (see figure 6.13, a and b).

If the linebacker is moving to the outside, the inside blocker should continue into the defensive lineman and use a hook block technique. The outside blocker in this case should continue to the outside and move up the field to block the linebacker with a drive block. When the linebacker charges straight ahead, the inside blocker should adjust his path to be in position to drive-block the linebacker with the inside shoulder. The outside blocker continues to hook-block the defensive lineman.

a

b

Figure 6.13   *(a-b)* Zone block.

Zone-Blocking Drill

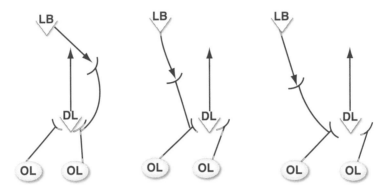

Players divide into groups of four with two offensive linemen (OL), who act as blockers, one defensive lineman (DL), and one linebacker (LB) as shown in the diagram. The two OL block the DL. To start the block, the OL that is directly in front of the DL uses the inside shoulder, arm, and hand, and the second blocker uses the shoulder, arm, and hand nearest the DL. Based on the LB and DL movement, one OL comes off the DL block to ensure that both the LB and the DL are blocked effectively.

Downfield Block Although most blocks occur near the line of scrimmage, blocking is needed in other situations. Receivers often need to block for their teammates in order to create space for them to run or to help them avoid a tackle. The downfield block is used in these situations. When using the downfield block, make sure the block is made above the defender's waist to avoid injury.

In a downfield block when the ball carrier is directly behind the blockers, they should use a run-block technique, which is a block made past the line of scrimmage on a defender who is trying to reach the ball carrier. In this situation, they block the defender at full or three-quarter speed by attacking aggressively with the forearms and shoulders (see figure 6.14). When blocking a

Figure 6.14   Downfield block.

Coaching Tip
Blockers should focus on and aim for a point 5 yards past the defensive player so that they learn to run through the block.

defensive player who is backing up, blockers should run straight through the block. Doing so creates space for the ball carrier, allowing him to pass the defender. If the defensive player is attacking up the field, blockers should block the player away from the ball carrier's path or in the direction he wants to go and let the defensive back cut off the block. Blockers should shorten their stride and widen their base as they near the defensive player.

If blockers have difficulty executing the downfield block, and the defensive player is avoiding the block, make certain that blockers are running under control with a shortened stride and are not leaning forward at the waist. Controlled body position and movement allow them to adjust their path at the last moment and make contact with the defensive player.

Downfield-Blocking Drill

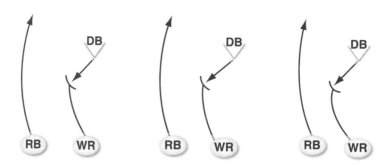

Players divide into groups of three with one wide receiver (WR), who acts as a blocker, one running back (RB), and one defensive back (DB) as shown in the diagram. The WR blocks the DB to allow the RB to run past the DB. The WR and DB start 5 yards apart. On the whistle, the WR charges toward the DB and aggressively blocks the DB with his forearms and shoulders while the DB tries to get through the block and tackle the RB.

Pass Protection Block   The pass protection block keeps the defender from getting to the quarterback before the quarterback can throw the football. The initial move and setup by an offensive lineman is extremely important in pass blocking. The offensive line player must set up quickly, stepping to the inside with the inside foot first, and must push up into a two-point stance with the down hand. The movement projects the offensive line player into a position with the head up, eyes open wide, back straight, rear end down, and hand and arms up. The player should position the feet shoulder-width apart with knees bent so that the body weight is maintained over the feet (see figure 6.15a). This allows backward or lateral movement in a split second, as shown in figure 6.15b. Elbows should be positioned into the side, and forearms and hands should be brought up with the palms open in front of the chest.

Coaching Tip
On defenses that allow a wide upfield rush by the defensive player, offensive tackles must learn that they may have to turn toward the sideline and force an outside rushing defensive player up the field past the quarterback's position.

The depth the pass blocker sets up off the line of scrimmage varies with the pass action called and the opponent's defensive front alignment and charge. Offensive linemen who are pass-blocking must position themselves between the quarterback and the defensive pass rusher. They can do this by backing off the line of scrimmage quickly after the snap. Tell your offensive line players that they should never be beaten to their inside. Offensive running backs who are pass-blocking must also position themselves between the quarterback and the defensive rusher, although they will be setting up a few yards deep in the backfield before the snap.

a   b

Figure 6.15   *(a-b)* Pass protection block.

Pass Protection Tips

Pass protection blocking is different from other blocks. Pass protection is different because the offensive player must sit and wait for the defensive player, rather than firing out aggressively on the snap of the ball. Following are a few helpful tips that coaches can use when teaching this block.

Punch

It takes good timing to deliver a blow to stop the charge of the defensive line player. The blocker must let the defensive line player get as close as six inches away from him and then deliver the blow to stop the charge. The blocker must strive to deliver a blow, step back from the defensive line player, and recoil. The blocker must deliver the punch with the elbows locked, keeping them held close to the rib cage. When delivering the punch, the blocker must also roll the wrists to achieve power. The blockers' hands and arms must stay within the planes of the shoulders.

When blockers lunge at the defensive player, make certain that they keep their back straight and do not bend forward at the waist, putting their head and shoulders in front of their hips. The forward lean makes it easier for the defensive player to move around the offensive blocker to reach the quarterback.

Patience

Patience quite possibly may be the hardest thing to teach offensive line players. Offensive line players must learn to be the protector, not the aggressor. They must keep their legs under them and must always remain in a good blocking position even after delivering the punch. Instruct offensive line players to keep their rear ends down and their knees bent at all times.

Footwork

The most important skill for offensive line players is the ability to move their feet. The correct foot movement is a shuffle, with the player keeping one foot always in contact with the ground. Offensive linemen should never cross their feet and should always keep their bodies between the defensive player and the quarterback with their backs always to the quarterback.

Pass Protection—Blocking Drill

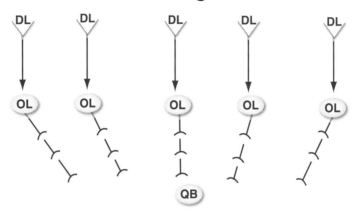

Offensive linemen (OL) act as blockers and line up directly in front of the defensive linemen (DL) as shown in the diagram. A cone or flag denoting the quarterback (QB) is positioned behind the OL. The coach moves down the line, calling out the snap count to each group. On the snap count from the coach, the DL rushes straight at the OL at half speed and does not take a side. The OL moves off the line and punches out with the arms and hands to block the approaching DL. The OL attempts to get into a position between the DL and the QB. The OL drives until the whistle is blown. Repeat the drill by resetting to hit out again.

A variation of this drill requires that it is performed the same as above, but the two outside OL face toward the sideline and push the DL up the field, wide of the QB. The three inside OL stay to the inside and in front of the DL, slow the charge, and force them wide of the QB.

Running the Ball

Running the ball involves many skills, including getting the handoff, carrying the ball, using blockers, and being the blocker. If much of your offense consists of running rather than passing plays, then developing the ability of your running backs to gain yardage is an important ingredient for your offensive team.

Getting the Handoff

Most running plays are designed for one of the running backs, rather than the quarterback, to carry the ball. Once quarterbacks take the ball from the center, their next job is to move into position so that they can hand off the ball to the running back. When running backs get the handoff from the quarterback, the elbow of the

Coaching Tip

When fumbles occur on the exchange, check the path of both players to the handoff point, the placement of the football by the quarterback, and the arm placement of the running back.

Figure 6.16   Proper handoff position.

arm closest to the quarterback should be raised to about shoulder level and bent at about 90 degrees with the forearm parallel to the ground and the palm turned toward the ground. The arm farthest from the quarterback should be flexed at the elbow with the forearm placed across the waist, the palm of the hand turned up, and the fingers spread in position to secure the ball. The quarterback is responsible for placing the ball firmly into the pocket formed by the running back's arms at the midsection, and the running back is responsible for securing the ball. If both players do their jobs, the handoff should be successful. Figure 6.16 shows a running back in proper handoff position.

On some running plays, the running back may not receive a direct handoff from the quarterback. Instead, the ball is pitched or tossed so that the running back can quickly get to the outside of the formation. The running back must look the ball into both hands and not run with the ball until it is caught. In preparing to catch the ball, the hands should be wide open with the little fingers together and palms up for a ball at waist level (see figure 6.17a) or with the thumbs together for a toss chest high (see figure 6.17b).

a   b

Figure 6.17   *(a-b)* Proper hand position when catching the pitch.

Upon making the catch, the running back should secure the ball and be prepared to make a cut and head up the field.

Carrying the Football

After receiving the ball, the running back must protect it at all cost. Teach ball carriers to immediately tuck the end of the ball under the arm and cover the front point of the ball with the hand as shown in figure 6.18. Coach your players to carry the ball in the arm away from the defense. When ball carriers run to the right, the ball should be in the right arm, and when they run to the left, the ball should be in the left arm.

> **Coaching Tip**
>
> When players fumble the ball, check to see if they are bringing the ball up away from the body as they run, if the ball is in the proper hand, and if the hand is placed firmly over the point of the ball.

Using Blockers

Coach your running backs to run toward the hole that has been called unless they see that it is closed. They should then head upfield to gain what yardage they can. Teach them to run with a forward lean. This helps them stay low and have a good forward drive.

Instruct the running backs to make their cut at the last moment. They should approach the line of scrimmage with their shoulders square to the line. To prevent the defender from getting a solid bead, a good running back will fake the defender by taking a step away from him and then cutting back close as if the ball carrier were cutting right through the defender. Coach running backs to set up their blockers by running on the blocker's outside hip, and then, at the last moment, cutting inside as the blocker blocks the defender.

Figure 6.18 Proper carrying position.

Being the Blocker

In addition to running with the ball, the running backs must also block for their teammates. On running plays, when the running backs are not running with the ball, they become blockers. As they near the defender, the blockers should widen their base, shorten their stride, and bend at the knees. When running backs are blockers on running plays, they should explode off the foot on the side of the shoulder that they're using to make the block. They should also keep their heads between the defender and the running back carrying the ball. Following are additional techniques for blocking:

- When a running back is not carrying the ball but is blocking on running plays, the running back uses a running drive block.

- When lead-blocking through the line, the blocker should head straight at the defensive player and try to run through the player with the block using the shoulder away from the desired path of the ball carrier.

- When blocking the end man on the line, the running back is required to make contact with the outside shoulder pad on the defender's inside hip for inside running plays or with the inside shoulder pad on the outside hip for any running play going wide.

Coaching Tip

When backs are sliding off their blocks, make sure that they have a wide base and that they are not turning their head away from the defender as they make contact.

In addition to blocking on running plays, running backs also need to block on passing plays. Pass protection blocking for a running back is different than for an offensive lineman because the defender takes time to reach the blocker. Running backs usually block linebackers who may rush from the outside or inside of the formation. In both situations, the first step of the running back should be a quick step to the inside with the inside foot.

When blocking an outside rusher, the running back will bring the outside foot around so that he is facing the sidelines and is in position to use the rusher's momentum and block the rusher up the field, past the quarterback. Blocking an inside rusher requires the running back to bring the outside foot even with the inside foot and be square to the line. From this position the running back can stop the rusher's charge and redirect the rusher to the outside or inside away from the quarterback's position. In both cases the running back should remember to do the following:

- Keep the feet shoulder-width apart.
- Keep the knees bent.
- Keep the back straight and head up.
- Keep the elbows in at the sides and both hands facing forward in front of the numbers with the palms facing forward.

When the rusher is about to make contact, the running back hits out hard with both hands, recoils, and then sets to hit out again.

When running backs miss a block, make certain that they are not leaning at the waist and are not lunging at the defensive pass rusher rather than setting and hitting out from a balanced position.

Running Back Blocking Drill

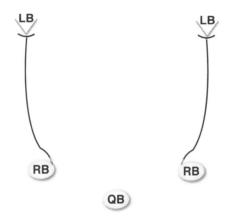

Two running backs (RB) act as blockers and each line up to the inside of two outside linebackers (LB) as shown in the diagram. A cone or flag denoting the quarterback (QB) is positioned behind and to the inside of the RBs. The RBs block one at a time and the coach indicates which RB blocks first. The RB blocks an LB to the outside and attempts to direct him toward the QB. The block should be made off the outside foot making contact with the outside shoulder on the RB's inside hip. Run the drill at half speed. Players return to their original starting positions after the run. Repeat the drill.

A variation of this drill requires the RB to block an inside linebacker to the outside and inside. The block should be made off the outside foot making contact with the outside shoulder on the RB's inside hip.

Playing Quarterback

Quarterbacks must be able to call the plays in the huddle and call out the cadence to start the play once the offense is positioned at the line of scrimmage and then execute the needed physical skills that the position demands. Quarterbacks also need to be mentally prepared to lead the offense. Quarterbacks should be taught the assignments of the entire offensive team once they have mastered this position. Quarterbacks must have a knowledge of the terminology used in calling plays and must act as a positive motivating force for the offense when it is on the field. Coaches must spend extra time with quarterbacks to make certain that they are prepared both physically and mentally. Teach your quarterbacks how to take snaps, play out of the shotgun formation, hand off, throw pitches and laterals, and throw passes.

Figure 6.19   Proper quarterback hand and arm positioning for the snap.

Coaching Tip

If quarterbacks are fumbling the ball, check to see if they are getting the snap correctly, if the ball is being brought up to their hands by the center, and if they are securing the ball into the body with both hands.

Taking the Snap

Offensive plays begin with the center handing or snapping the ball to the quarterback. For an offensive play to be successful, the exchange of the ball from the center to the quarterback must be executed in a smooth motion.

In a tight formation, quarterbacks should place their throwing hand, or pressure hand, so that it pushes up on the center's rear end. This pressure tells the center where to snap the football. Quarterbacks should position the bottom hand, or catch hand, so that the thumbs are together and the fingers extended, giving the center a good target for the ball as shown in figure 6.19. Quarterbacks should bend their elbows slightly to allow for the center's firing out on the snap. Quarterbacks must adjust their stance to the height of the center.

Figure 6.20 illustrates a quarterback receiving the snap. Quarterbacks look downfield as the snap is being made and, after receiving the snap, immediately turn their head to see where to hand off the ball. When quarterbacks locate their target, they should keep their eyes on that player. On passing plays, they bring the football into the body at the chest and then raise it up and back to the ear in a

Figure 6.20   Quarterback receiving the snap.

ready-to-throw position. Quarterbacks should not swing the football away from the body when moving to make a handoff or dropping to pass.

Coordination between the center and quarterback is essential. Inconsistent snaps may be caused by the quarterback moving in the opposite direction of the center, who is moving to make a block while snapping the ball. The quarterback must know where the center is moving and follow the center's movement until the ball is secure. Practice the center's blocking movement during your regular practices.

Shotgun Formation

Quarterbacks start in the shotgun formation—that is, about 5 to 7 yards behind the center, depending on the particular play or their arm strength. They should look at the defense and scan the field for particular defensive formations. This enables them to see who might be open or alerts them to call an audible if the defensive set indicates that a change of play is needed. An important key when using a shotgun formation, too, is a center who can accurately snap the ball to the quarterback the necessary 5 to 7 yards.

Handoff

On all offensive plays where the running back will carry the ball, the quarterback must get the ball to the running back after taking the snap from the center. Quarterbacks are completely responsible for the success or failure of the handoff. They must adjust to the running back's path and speed and get him the football. Quarterbacks should keep both hands on the ball as long as possible and place or press the ball firmly into the ball carrier's abdomen, allowing the give hand to ride the ball into place until the running back takes it.

Coaching Tip
Failure to complete the handoff is often caused when the quarterback is too close or too far away from the running back when attempting to make the handoff. Review the footwork needed by both players for proper positioning on each play.

Pitches and Laterals

Quarterbacks should use a two-hand push pass or an underhand toss on all pitch plays (see figure 6.21). Quarterbacks need this skill for running plays when there is no time to hand the ball to the running back. This will usually be an offensive running play where the running back starts immediately to the sidelines and catches the ball while running to the outside of the formation. The quarterback must learn to pitch or toss the ball in front of the running back so that the running back is not forced to slow down to make the catch.

A pitch play or a toss play is a lateral, not a forward pass. It is thrown either to the side or back—in relation to the line of scrimmage—rather than forward. A dropped lateral is not an incomplete pass. It is a fumble, and either the offense or the defense can recover and gain possession of the ball.

a   b

Figure 6.21   Quarterback executing *(a)* the two-hand push pass and *(b)* the underhand toss when making the pitch.

Throwing the Football

To successfully throw the ball, the quarterback must master four skills: grip, throwing position, release, and follow-through. Even if the other 10 offensive players do their jobs correctly, if the quarterback cannot accurately throw the ball to the intended receiver, the passing segment of the offense will not be successful.

Figure 6.22   Proper grip for the quarterback with the ball in the ready position.

Grip   Quarterbacks should spread their fingers over the laces of the ball and hold the ball slightly behind the center position on the ball with a secure grip. Quarterbacks keep the ball in the ready position close to their armpit before raising it straight up to throw. Figure 6.22 shows the proper grip with the ball in the ready position.

Throwing Position   Quarterbacks should bring the ball with both hands to the throwing position just behind the ear (see figure

6.23a) and move the nonpassing hand away and in front of the ball (see figure 6.23b). The upper part of the passing arm should be about parallel to the ground with the nonpassing shoulder (left shoulder for a right-handed passer) pointing to the intended receiver. Legs should be about shoulder-width apart with the weight partially on the back foot.

a   b

Figure 6.23   *(a-b)* Proper throwing position for a quarterback.

Release   Quarterbacks should start the throwing motion with their legs by stepping directly at the target with the front foot then bringing the hips and shoulders in line with the direction of the front foot. Good passers use their legs as much as their arm to throw. They step at the target and rotate the body so that the hips and chest face the target as the arm comes through. The ball should be thrown from behind the ear (see figure

Coaching Tip

Errors in accuracy can be a result of quarterbacks not moving the entire body toward the target as they throw passes. Make certain that quarterbacks push off the back foot and step at the receiver rather than simply setting up and using arm action to deliver the ball.

6.24), released with a strong wrist snap and with the palm turned down toward the ground. As the ball is released, the fingers should drag across it to cause it to spiral. The index finger is the last to leave the ball and should be pointed directly toward the target. The quarterback's entire body should move directly toward the receiver as the ball is released.

Follow-Through   Quarterbacks should not lower the passing arm down across the body too quickly after releasing the ball. Instead, they should try to make the hand "follow the ball" to the target and rotate the passing hand so that the palm points to the ground (see figure 6.25).

Figure 6.24   Proper release positioning for a quarterback.

Figure 6.25   Proper follow-through for a quarterback.

Drop-Back Pass

Next quarterbacks must learn how to apply proper throwing technique to a game or gamelike practice situation. When quarterbacks take the snap from the center and drop back to pass, they vary their steps based on the distance of the receivers' pass routes as they run down the field. Short passes require a three-step drop, and medium to deep pass routes require a five-step drop before throwing the ball. The quarterbacks' last step should stop their movement away from the center and allow them to set up to step and throw.

Quarterback Three- and Five-Step Drop-Back Drill

A quarterback (QB) and center (C) line up as shown in the diagram. The C has the ball and, on the coach's command, hands the ball to the QB to start the drill. If a C is not available, the coach can hand the ball to the QB. Once the ball is handed to the QB, the QB executes a three- or five-step drop with the ball in both hands and number high as he starts the drop. The QB stops the three-step drop with the third step and is prepared to step and throw. The QB stops the five-step drop with an elongated fifth step, comes under control, and is prepared to step and throw. For the five-step drop, if field conditions are bad, the QB should shorten the final step and keep the feet under his hips.

Receiving

Receiving involves running disciplined pass patterns—pass routes—and catching the football when the quarterback throws it. Wide receivers are an important part of your offensive attack. They need to understand that they can make big contributions to helping the offense move down the field and score.

Running Patterns or Routes

When the quarterback calls a play in the huddle, the receiver learns what pass route to run to complete the play. The quarterback selects a play that uses routes from many options on what is called a "pass tree." Because a receiver runs a variety of pass routes and different depths from the line of scrimmage, offensive coaches have designed these routes to resemble a tree with each route representing a branch. The pass tree is discussed in more detail in the "Passing Game" section on pages 100 to 101.

The most important thing to teach receivers about running pass routes is to explode off the line of scrimmage. This allows receivers to immediately drive down

Coaching Tip

Teach receivers the exact distance they should run up the field before they reach the breaking point and the distance they will usually travel before the ball reaches them at the receiving point. Practicing these routes over and over helps receivers instinctively know how far to run and where the ball should be when they catch it during a game.

the field and forces the defensive back—who is trying to keep the receiver from catching the ball—to start running away from the line of scrimmage. When running routes, receivers should run to the outside shoulder of the defensive back, forcing defenders to turn their shoulders parallel to the line of scrimmage to cover them. Once defenders turn their body, it is easy for the receiver to run a pass route in the opposite direction or to stop and quickly turn back to the quarterback to make the catch.

Breaking- and Receiving-Points Drill

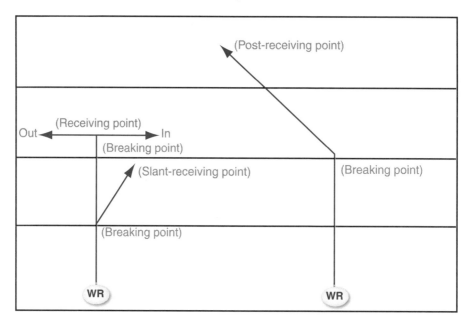

Two wide receivers (WR) line up on a designated yard line as shown in the diagram. The coach determines the type of pass route to be used and instructs the WR to run specified routes one at a time without a ball. For short (5 yards) and medium (10 to 12 yards) routes coming to the center of the field, the WR runs 6 yards after the break before the ball arrives and 8 to 10 yards on patterns to the outside. On deep patterns (more than 12 yards), the WR's receiving point should be extended by 3 to 4 yards. The coach should stress the need to keep the breaking point constant for every route and to keep running to reach the receiving point. The WRs return to the original starting positions after running the route. Repeat the drill.

Receivers must also come under control at the breaking point—the point a certain distance off the line of scrimmage where they stop running straight up the field—and adjust their path to move in the direction of the pass route called in the huddle. At this point in the pass route, they lean their upper body in the direction they want to go next. They should roll over the foot on the side of the body in the direction they are headed, turn the head and shoulders, and react to the football. They should anticipate catching the ball after they have adjusted their pass route. The point where receivers make the catch is termed the "receiving point." The distance receivers run to achieve the receiving point varies depending on the pass route they are running and the timing of the pass from the quarterback.

Catching the Football

Properly catching the football is a matter of concentration and dedication. First and foremost, receivers should always watch the football into their hands. If the football is thrown high, receivers should catch it with thumbs together and their wrist cocked slightly back (see figure 6.26a); if it is thrown low, receivers should catch it with little fingers together and their palms up (see figure 6.26b).

Coaching Tip

When players are slow coming out of their break, it is usually because they have planted a foot, which stops their momentum so they have to start moving all over again. Coach players to lean with the upper body in the direction that they want to go and to roll over the foot on that side. This maneuver allows them to keep their momentum through the entire pass route.

a

b

Figure 6.26 Receiver catching *(a)* a high ball and *(b)* a low ball.

Receivers should catch the football in their hands without trapping it against their bodies. Receivers should work on reaching out with both hands toward the ball when making a catch so that they can see both hands and the ball at the moment of the reception (see figure 6.27). Receivers should then tuck the ball under the arm and protect it after making the catch.

Figure 6.27   Receiver preparing to catch the ball with the hands away from the body.

Coaching Tip
Dropped passes usually occur when receivers don't have their hands together and don't reach for the ball and when they take their eyes off the ball at the moment of the catch. Check all three areas if receivers drop passes, and explain the importance of each part of the receiving motion in making the catch.

Give receivers ample opportunities in practice to catch the types of passes they will see in games. As a coach, you cannot expect athletes to perform skills in a game that they have not worked on in practice. Success will help the receivers gain confidence, and first downs and touchdowns reinforce that catching the ball is fun.

Centering the Ball

Players at the center position must learn how to bring the ball up from the ground to the quarterback's hands—called "centering the ball"—in both a tight formation and in a shotgun formation.

In the tight formation, the quarterback lines up directly behind the center with the hands open and ready to receive the ball directly from the center. At one point in the ball exchange, both the center's hands and the quarterback's hands will touch the ball (see figure 6.20 on page 86). The snap should be hard and direct, going through the center's legs and into the quarterback's waiting hands. For beginning centers, it is often easier to start in a four-point offensive line stance as shown in figure 6.1 on page 63 and then place the ball under the player's snapping hand. This places the ball slightly in front of and just to the inside of the center's shoulder pad.

In the shotgun formation, the center snaps the ball through the legs to the quarterback, who is 5 to 7 yards behind the line of scrimmage. The snap should be crisp, but not so fast that it is hard to handle. The ball should reach the quarterback from the belt line to the middle of the chest, with a nice spiral so that it is easy to grab. The center should look between the legs to place the quarterback and then bring the head up before the snap.

Centers should first practice snapping the ball to the quarterback slowly, making sure they are placing it properly with the laces at or near the fingers of the quarterback's throwing hand. The players should then practice at full speed. Spend five minutes each day on center–quarterback exchanges. Once the snap is secure, have centers move either straight ahead or to the right or left or set to pass-block while making the exchange like they would in a game.

Coaching Tip

If centers have trouble blocking a player directly in front of them or to the side of their snapping hand, have them take a short lateral step with the foot on the side of the snapping hand. This moves a portion of the body in front of the defender and allows them time to get both hands into position to block.

Offensive Tactics

Once your team understands and can properly execute the individual offensive technical skills, they can begin putting them together into offensive schemes, or tactics. The plays you teach your offense will comprise your offensive tactics, or your "game plan." When designing offensive tactics, start with plays, either running or passing, that use the skills your team has mastered. (When working with beginners, running the ball is usually easier to teach because handing off is a simpler skill than the throwing and catching required for the passing game.) Remember that the key to tactical success is using plays that optimize your players' strengths. For example, if your quarterback can pass accurately and your receivers can catch the ball, feature offensive tactics that highlight passing. Conversely, if blocking and running the ball are your team's strengths, your game plan should feature running plays.

The objectives you set for your team's offensive tactics must be realistic and important—not just to you, but also to your players. If your team is incapable of reaching the goals, or is not interested in achieving them, they serve little purpose. It may seem that scoring is the most obvious and most important objective when a team is on offense, but scoring is merely an outcome produced by the team's ability to achieve three goals. The following are the three most important goals an offensive team can strive to accomplish:

1. *Execute consistently.*

   To execute consistently, you must run the same plays throughout the season and work on them continually. Select a simple offense that has some deception and teach it well. A few well-executed plays can give even the best opponents all they can handle. If your offense uses too many plays, chances are your team members, not your opponents, will be confused.

Consistent execution stems from your athletes' understanding the plays and practicing them repeatedly. Every player must know what is expected of him for each play. Teaching assignments is not enough. Equal time must be spent teaching every player the techniques they need to carry out their assignment.

Practicing these plays against the defense that you expect opponents to play will help your players visualize the way they should run each play. If your players know that a team goal is consistent execution, they'll be more eager to perform the plays as often as necessary to make them work in a game. Teach your receivers the proper patterns to run and your quarterback the proper depth to drop to throw the football. Your players need to practice running a pattern many times before they'll feel confident that it will work. Develop a game plan early in the week and then simplify it so that on game day you have only a handful of plays. By using a limited number of plays each week and giving the players enough repetitions to eliminate mistakes, you'll help your team execute consistently.

2. *Move the football.*

The object on offense is to move down the field and score by using a good mix of running and passing plays. Running basic plays against the defense you anticipate seeing is the best way to prepare your team to move the football in a game. The offense must believe that it can march the football down the field regardless of the team they're playing or the defense they're facing. Select plays that use the strengths of your offense and expose the defense's weakness.

3. *Maintain possession.*

Obviously, when the offense controls the football, the opponent cannot score. To keep control, the offense must consistently produce first downs and eliminate turnovers by protecting the football. An offensive game plan with effective running plays combined with short, quick passes is hard to stop. Using a good mix of plays keeps the chains moving steadily toward the opponent's goal line. Maintaining possession is especially important when your team has a narrow lead at the end of a game. The other team can't score if it doesn't have the ball.

Coaching Tip

Emphasize to your offense to think first in terms of making first downs and then to envision making touchdowns. It is important to take small steps toward the larger goal.

To execute, move the ball, and maintain possession, you must have a balanced attack that features a strong running game and a complementary passing game based on the ability of your quarterback to keep the defense off balance. Also important to a strong offensive game is an offensive numbering system and effective use of the hurry-up offense.

Running Game

When developing an effective running game, the most important step is to design plays in which the blocking and backfield action work together and cause indecision and confusion for the defense. The backfield action on any play must be designed to put the running back at the point of attack just as the hole is opening. Three types of blocks can help accomplish this: fast or quick blocking on straight-ahead plays (see figure 6.28), fold blocking on slower-hitting plays (see figure 6.29), and power blocking on sweeps (see figure 6.30).

You should also set up the running game so that it is effective and easy to communicate. The simplest way to communicate running plays is to number each hole—the natural gaps between the offensive blockers—and the running back as shown in figure 6.31 on page 99. The running back runs the ball into the hole that is called. For example, play 32 means that the number 3 running back runs the ball through the number 2 hole. It is easier and quicker in both practice and games to call out 32, for example, than to specify that the running back runs through the gap between the guard and center.

In developing a running game, consider the different series of plays that can be successful. All series should include built-in dimension—that part of a given series that provides variation for backfield movement. Dimension will

Figure 6.28 Fast or quick block for straight-ahead plays.

Figure 6.29 Fold block for slower-hitting plays.

Figure 6.30 Power block for sweeps.

make it difficult for the defense to determine the point of attack when the ball is snapped, which forces the defense to respect your entire attack. An example of a series is a dive 30 and a trap 30. These both involve the number 3 running back running through the hole right in the center of the line, but the running back gets there using different actions and the blocking is different.

The running game should give you the opportunity to run the football in every offensive hole. By incorporating a series of plays, you'll be able to run

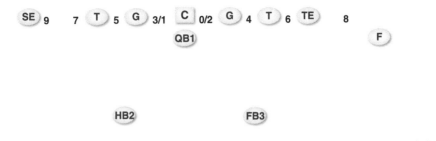

Figure 6.31 Numbering holes and running backs.

the various holes in more than one way. The game plan, however, should include only four or five running plays chosen from the total series of plays. These are the plays you will perfect for a given opponent.

Successful football teams use runs that are effective against the opponent they are playing. For example, if the defense is coming across the line of scrimmage very hard, you would use the trap series. Against a hard-charging defense, it is easier for offensive line players to get an angle if a trap is called. Sometimes defenders take themselves out of (overrun) the play; other times they can be blocked from the side. Against a reading defense, the dive and sweep would be effective. If the defense stacks the line of scrimmage and has more defensive people on the line than you have blockers, you may be better off throwing the ball.

The running backs are an integral part of a good running offense. Coach them to gain yardage on every play. They should be competitive and have the desire to be successful. Running backs who are hard to tackle and who keep their feet driving will create more touchdowns.

Coaching Tip

If the plays you're calling during a game don't seem to be effective, have an assistant write down every play you call and record the result. Then refer to this call sheet to determine which plays produce the best results.

Passing Game

If you have a quarterback who can throw the ball well and a couple of good receivers who can catch it consistently, then the passing game would be a nice addition to your offensive scheme. The forward pass is a potent way to gain yardage and score points. Throwing the football helps develop individual players, forces the defense to defend the whole field, gains yardage on offense, and appeals to the crowd.

To effectively execute passing plays, you must do a good job of drilling the quarterbacks and receivers in the basic skills covered earlier in this chapter. They must be well versed in throwing and catching the ball. You must also be sure that your team understands pass protection and appropriate blocking techniques.

Keep the passing attack simple so that the quarterbacks and receivers know what to do. Timing is important to the success of a passing attack, so you must allow time in practice for players to perform many repetitions of the basic patterns. Also, with young quarterbacks, you must not ask them to throw pass routes that they do not have the ability to throw. When your team has trouble completing passes, make certain that the pass is timed properly to the route the receiver is running and the distance the quarterback drops when setting up to throw.

The passing game starts with a pass tree as shown in figure 6.32. These are patterns that the receivers run to get open to catch the football. The quarterback drops straight back (or rolls out) and throws the football to the open receiver. The passing game takes time to develop, and you must be patient in bringing the separate parts of this offense together. Here are the pass patterns we recommend, as are shown in figure 6.32, that you can teach your players:

- Hitch — The hitch pattern is run at 5 yards. The receiver should run straight down the field and then quickly turn back to the inside to make the catch.

- Quick out — The quick-out pattern is very successful when the defensive player is playing off the receiver and to the inside. The receiver runs downfield 5 yards and then cuts sharply to the sideline, catching the ball just before stepping out of bounds.

- Slant — The slant pattern is a quick pattern where the receiver runs straight down the field for 5 yards and then angles in at a 45-degree angle to the center of the field and the quarterback takes three steps and throws.

- Out — The out pattern is a pattern run in the 10 to 12 yard area where the receiver runs straight down the field and then breaks sharply to the sideline.

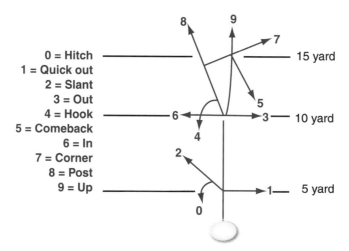

0 = Hitch
1 = Quick out
2 = Slant
3 = Out
4 = Hook
5 = Comeback
6 = In
7 = Corner
8 = Post
9 = Up

15 yard

10 yard

5 yard

Figure 6.32   Pass tree.

- Hook — When the defensive player retreats too fast or is playing off the receiver and to the outside, use the curl pattern. The receiver drives deep for 10 to 12 yards and then curls back to the football.

- Comeback—The comeback is a pattern that is run off of the up pattern. The receiver bends to the outside at 10 yards, starts straight up the field for 5 yards and then breaks sharply to the outside coming back toward the line of scrimmage to make the reception.

- In — The in pattern is also run at 10 to 12 yards and is the opposite of the out pattern. The receiver runs straight down the field and then breaks sharply to the center of the field. The receiver should keep running across the field.

- Corner — The corner is similar to a post, except the receiver starts into the post for four steps and then breaks to the outside at an angle, toward a corner of the field.

- Post — The post is similar to the up pattern in that it is a deep pattern. At 10 yards the receiver breaks deep to the inside at an angle toward the center of the field.

- Up — Use the up pattern if the defensive back is playing tight on a receiver with speed. The receiver runs up the field 10 yards, bends to the outside, and then sprints straight up the field on the outside of the defensive back.

Hurry-Up Offense

Whether you are using running or passing plays, the hurry-up offense is a powerful tactical weapon. The hurry-up offense moves the ball quickly down the field without huddles. This means focusing on a combination of your one or two running plays and your best passing plays, some short and some long. Players can line up at the line without a huddle and the quarterback can call out the play to be run. The snap count should be the same for most plays during a hurry-up offense.

If your team has trouble running a no-huddle offense, make certain that the quarterback is letting each offensive player get set. Also consider limiting the offense to fewer plays that can be called by a "live" color. When the offensive players hear the live color, they know that the next play called at the line by the quarterback is the one they should run. The live color can be changed from week to week if necessary or can remain the same throughout the year because the offense faces a new team each week.

7

Coaching Defense

Defensive players begin every play at a disadvantage. While offensive players know which play they will run and when it will begin, defensive players are waiting for the offensive center to snap the ball so they can quickly try to determine which play the offense is attempting to run, react to the play, and try to get in on the tackle.

The role of the defensive team is to stop the offense. They can do this by denying the offense a first down (forcing them to give up the ball), by making them punt the ball, by recovering a fumble, or by making an interception. And finally the defense must also think about scoring. Playing defense is part instinct, part effort, and part technique. You, as a coach, can improve your players' instincts through teaching technique, practicing plays, and repetition. This chapter focuses on the defensive techniques and tactics—plays—that your players must learn to succeed in youth football.

Defense Must Be Fun

Defensive football players are the aggressive kids who love to run and make contact. If you encourage emotion in defensive players, they will become excited when they make a tackle, recover a fumble, or intercept a pass. This excitement adds to team unity, and the players will perform at a higher level. Encourage team tackling, with everyone pursuing the ball until the whistle blows. This motivates defensive players to swarm the ball carrier and adds to team spirit. Stress hard work in an attempt to gain success, but make sure you add fun to the game.

Defensive Techniques

The defensive team is made up of the defensive line, the linebackers, and then the defensive backs. Each group of players performs specific tasks and must master the skills needed for their position. These basic skills are an integral part of all defensive football, serving as the foundation your players will build on to play well at all levels. The basics your defensive players must master are assuming the defensive stance, defeating blockers, tackling, rushing the passer, and covering receivers.

Stance

The proper initial alignment of the body for the defensive player is key to reacting instantly and being able to effectively play the defense. Teach the defensive line players—linebackers and defensive backs—the proper stances for their respective positions. Be sure to emphasize to defensive players that they must move out of their stance immediately when the ball is snapped in order to counter the advantage the offense has of knowing where the ball is going and when the play will begin.

Defensive Line

The typical stance for defensive line players is similar to the offensive line player's three-point stance (see figure 6.2 on page 63). However, some defensive line players are more comfortable with the outside hand on the ground, creating a four-point stance as shown in figure 7.1.

When in either stance, players should place more weight on their hands so that they can move forward and should use a stance that is a little wider than the offensive stance so that they have better balance when they're being blocked. Players should keep their outside hand (the hand away from the blocker) free to try pass rush techniques and to keep from getting hooked. The player's body must be low to the ground and must control the line of scrimmage from under the opponent's shoulder pads.

Linebackers

Linebackers should have a good balanced stance, which means that their feet are shoulder-width apart and slightly staggered (see figure 7.2). The knees should be bent slightly to ensure low body position with the hands near the upper thighs. Their eyes are focused on the player that they will get the "cue" from. One foot is slightly forward and linebackers step with this foot first as they react to the key and find the football.

If linebackers are catching the blocker, this often occurs because they have their shoulder in front of their

Figure 7.1   Four-point stance for defensive linemen.

Figure 7.2   Proper stance for linebackers.

Coaching Tip

Defensive linemen with their feet behind their hips in their stance typically rise up, rather than move forward on the snap of the ball. This makes them easier to block. If you see defensive linemen standing straight up, have them move into their stance and watch to see if they move their feet back as they place their hands on the ground. Correct them immediately and have them place their hands on the ground without adjusting the foot position.

hips and feet, which forces them to lean into the blocker. Teach linebackers to stand in a more upright stance with their shoulders only slightly in front of their hips.

Defensive Backs

Defensive backs should line up with a slightly staggered stance in a relaxed position as shown in figure 7.3a. Before the play starts, the defensive backs should position their heads so that they can look to the ball and see the start of the play. Their shoulders should be in front of their hips, and their arms and hands can hang down in a relaxed position.

Corners keep their feet slightly staggered, with the inside foot back (see figure 7.3b). They should bring their outside foot to the center of the body so that it is on the ground in line under the chin, and the foot should be turned so that they can push off the side of the foot and not just the toes. Corners should push off their front foot and take a step back at the start of each play.

a   b   c

Figure 7.3 Proper stance for *(a)* defensive backs *(b)* corners, and *(c)* free safeties.

Free safeties line up with a square stance (see figure 7.3c), and strong safeties line up with a slightly staggered stance similar to corners as shown in figure 7.3b. The toes are pointed straight ahead and the players should assume a slightly crouched position with the knees slightly bent. Eyes are focused on the player that the safety will "key" from. Safeties can take a short read step on the snap, and then react to the play.

Defeating Blockers

Every defensive player needs to understand the importance of defeating an offensive blocker before locating the offensive player with the ball and moving to be part of the tackle. A defensive lineman or linebacker's first indication that the offense will run the ball is when the offensive linemen aggressively attack across the line of scrimmage the moment the ball is snapped. In that instant, defensive players must determine who the blocker will be if they are to defeat the block.

For the defensive linemen, the blocker will be close, directly in front of them, or to one side or the other. Linebackers who are lined up off the line will have more time to determine who is going to block them. Defensive backs, who are lined up the farthest off the line of scrimmage will easily see who is assigned to block them on each play.

Once defensive players have determined the offensive player assigned to block them, they need to attack by stepping into the blocker, keeping their shoulder pads below the blocker's pads. In the case of the defensive linemen, as they step to meet the blocker, they need to bring up their forearm into the blocker's body as their shoulder pad makes contact. Once the blocker's momentum has been stopped, the defensive players need to push the offensive player away and off the block with their other hand, locate the player running with the ball, and move in that direction to make the tackle. A linebacker may have the chance to use the same forearm technique to defeat the blocker if the blocker raises up as he comes off the line of scrimmage. Linebackers and defensive backs may find that the blocker is lower than they are in their stance so they will need to defeat the blocker by extending both arms and stopping the blocker by hitting out with the palms of both hands into the shoulder pads of the blocker.

> **Coaching Tip**
> The receiver often reaches the defensive back too quickly if the defensive back steps forward on the first step rather than back. Emphasize to defensive backs to push off their front foot and take a first step back with their back foot, stepping so that they start their momentum away from the receiver they want to cover.

> **Coaching Tip**
> If a defensive player is continually getting blocked, often it is because the player is looking into the backfield, trying to find out who has the ball rather than locating and defeating the blocker first.

Figure 7.4   Proper hitting position.

Tackling

If you want to have a good defensive team, you must teach your defensive players how to tackle. As the players grow and progress to learn the game, it is important to teach them the proper tackling techniques. When first introducing your players to tackling, it is important to start at half speed until they master the correct technique and feel comfortable with the contact associated with making a tackle.

Tacklers should always be in the proper hitting position with their head up, back straight, knees bent, and feet shoulder-width apart as shown in figure 7.4. They should also focus on a target when making the tackle—generally the area near the runner's belt buckle. If tacklers always focus on this target, their opponents will not be able to fake them out with a fancy shoulder move, head fake, or spin maneuver.

It is important to note that all tackles should be made with the shoulder pad and never with the helmet. You must stress to your players that they always keep their head up and eyes open and position their body so that they tackle with one shoulder pad or the other and never with their head.

The three basic tackles that your players will use are the head-on tackle, the angle tackle, and the open-field tackle. Following are coaching points for each type.

Head-On Tackle

Defensive players use the head-on tackle when they line up straight across from the offensive runner coming toward them. Tacklers should first make sure that they are in a good hitting position and are ready to make the tackle.

Tacklers must maintain a wide, balanced stance while keeping the feet moving with choppy steps. The back is arched and the knees are slightly bent. The head and arms should extend in front of the body, and the head should be up. A head-on tackle means that the ball carrier is coming straight toward the tackler; it does not mean that tacklers lead with the head! Be sure that tacklers slide their head to the outside before making contact.

When executing the head-on tackle, tacklers explode off of the foot on the same side as the shoulder with which they will make the tackle. They drive their shoulder into the runner's abdomen as they thrust their hips through as shown in figure 7.5. With their arms, they grasp behind the legs of the ball carrier and pull the player toward them, lifting and pulling the ball carrier toward them as they take them off their feet. Tacklers should remain under control so that they don't overrun the ball carrier or dive and miss the tackle.

When players miss tackles, make sure they have widened their feet and shortened their stride and they are bending their knees and not leaning forward at the waist.

Figure 7.5 Proper head-on tackling technique.

Head On—Tackling Drill

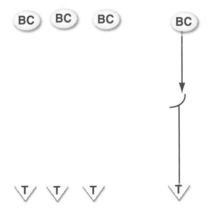

Players are divided into two groups and positioned as shown in the diagram: one group of ball carriers (BC) and one group of tacklers (T). On the coach's command, the first BC in line and the first T in line start toward each other at half speed. At 5 yards, the T explodes off the left foot and makes contact with the BC with the left shoulder pad to make the tackle. The T must remember to keep the head up and not tackle with the helmet. Players switch lines after each player has had a turn.

Angle Tackle

The angle tackle is necessary when the ball carrier runs a wide play or gets close to the sideline. Tacklers must first make sure that they are in a good hitting position and must maintain a good balanced stance when preparing for this tackle.

When executing the angle tackle, tacklers must drive the head in front of the ball carrier's number, across the line of his run, and drive the shoulder upward on the runner at about waist level (see figure 7.6). When players are angle-tackling with the ball carrier breaking to their right, for example, they use the left shoulder pad to make the tackle and explode off of the left foot. The back should be arched to lift and drive through the ball carrier. With the arms, they should grasp the runner behind the legs and lift him off the ground and keep the feet moving with short, choppy steps as they finish the tackle. Tacklers should remain under control and ready to move in any direction.

Coaching Tip

If players have trouble getting their head in front of the ball carrier, check to see that they are taking off with the correct foot. Players should use the shoulder pad and foot on the same side when making the tackle.

Figure 7.6 Angle tackle.

Angle-Tackling Drill

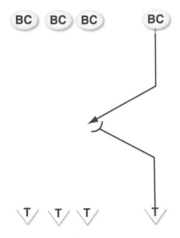

Players are divided into two groups and positioned as shown in the diagram: one group of ball carriers (BC) and one group of tacklers (T). On the coach's command, the first BC in line and the first T in line start toward each other at half speed. At 5 yards, the BC breaks at an angle to his right. The T breaks to his left at the same time. The T explodes off of the right foot and makes contact with the right shoulder pad to make the tackle. Players switch lines after each player has had a turn.

Open-Field Tackle

After the runner has cleared the line of scrimmage or when a receiver has caught the football and has just one player to beat, defensive players must make an open-field tackle. Tacklers should learn that the most important thing to do in the open field is to get hold of the opponent and pull him the ground (see figure 7.7). In the stance, tacklers must remain under control with their legs bent, head up, and back straight and be prepared to move in any direction.

When executing the open-field tackle, tacklers should remember that their number-one priority is to grasp the runner. They should use the sideline to their advantage,

Figure 7.7   Open-field tackle.

penning in or getting an angle on the runner. Once they have a hold on the runner, help should soon arrive. But, if possible, they should try to drive the ball carrier out of bounds or pull him to the turf. Tacklers shouldn't worry about driving through the player or delivering a hard blow. The sole responsibility is to get hold of the player and prevent the score.

Players who must tackle a ball carrier in the open field often lunge at and miss the ball carrier. Remind them to be patient, make certain where the ball carrier is going, and then commit by opening up and stepping with the foot on the side of the direction of the ball carrier's movement.

Rushing the Passer

When the offense runs the ball, they use aggressive blocking when the play begins. And when they're going to pass the ball, the offensive blockers sit back rather than firing out. Defensive linemen must recognize this change and immediately think about charging across the line to put pressure on—or rush—the quarterback. At this time, defensive players must determine which offensive blocker will block them. On the pass, they must defeat that block before looking for the quarterback.

To improve the pass rush of the defensive line players, teach them to know where the quarterback will set up and encourage them to plan their pass rush technique before the play begins. If defensive players have an idea of which pass rush technique they will use as they charge from their stance, the greater their chance of defeating the pass protection block and reaching the quarterback.

When teaching pass rush techniques to young players, teach only a few techniques that your players can perfect. Defensive players can put pressure on—or rush—the quarterback in three ways: the bull rush technique, the rip or swim technique, and the spin technique.

Coaching Tip

If players using a bull rush are blocked right at the line of scrimmage, make sure they drive their feet with short, choppy steps; have good forward lean; and have a wide base. This continued forward charge will ensure that they move across the line of scrimmage and force the blocker back into the area where the quarterback is setting up to throw.

Bull Rush Technique

A bull rush occurs when the defensive player controls the offensive blocker by locking both arms into the offensive blocker's armpits, and, with the leverage provided by locking the elbows, lifts the offensive line player up, forcing the blocker back into the quarterback (see figure 7.8). This type of rush requires good arm and hand strength.

Rip or Swim Technique

In the rip or swim pass rush technique, the defensive player moves around the offensive blocker and then attacks the quarterback. The rip and the swim movements are similar; the

Figure 7.8   Bull rush.

arm farthest from the blocker repositions the blocker, while the arm closest to the blocker creates the movement for the defensive player to move past the blocker.

In the rip technique, the defender moves the forearm up and under the blocker's arm (see figure 7.9a) in an attempt to knock the blocker off balance and allow the defensive player to move around the blocker. If the defensive player is going to his right, he uses the left arm to "rip." The right arm should push the blocker's left arm up and back. As the left arm rips, it is important to step by the blocker with the left leg.

In the swim technique, the defender extends the arm and "swims" over the top of the blocker (see figure 7.9b). If the defensive player is going to his

a   b

Figure 7.9   *(a)* Rip or *(b)* swim technique.

right, he uses the left arm to swim. The right arm should push the blocker's left arm down and in. As the left arm swims, it is important to step by the blocker with the left leg. Once the arm is over the blocker, the defender pushes off and moves toward the quarterback. The swim motion and the push-off should be one continuous movement.

Players who have trouble making contact and directing the blocker's arm on the side of the pass rush and getting past the blocker with either the rip or the swim technique often start the move too far away from the blocker or use the wrong technique for the opponent. It is often more effective for a shorter defensive player to use the rip technique. A taller player often has more success using the swim technique. Try to match the physical stature of your players with the pass rush technique that will work best for them.

Pass Rush Drill

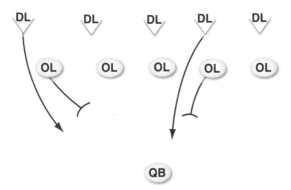

Players divide into two groups of five defensive line (DL) players and five offensive line (OL) players positioned directly across from each other as shown in the diagram. Another player acts as the quarterback (QB) and is positioned as shown in the diagram. The coach indicates a pass rush technique and indicates which DL and OL go first. The coach signals the snap count to the offensive player and calls out a cadence to start the drill. On the coach's command, the DL pass rushes the QB until the whistle is blown. The DL and OL start at half speed until they have mastered the pass rush techniques. Players rush one at a time to avoid injury, and the coach should work on one technique at a time. Players switch positions after the rush is completed. Repeat drill.

Spin Technique

In the spin technique, rushers use their hands and arms to spin the blocker and get into the offensive backfield. The defender spins a full 360 degrees in getting around the blocker. The defenders should start the spin by moving in close to the blocker, hitting the blocker in the chest with the forearm on the side of their spin, and then throwing the opposite leg and arm around as the forearm pushes off the blocker.

Blockers can adjust their position to make a block if players don't make solid contact with the blocker and try to spin from too far a distance. Defensive players using this technique to rush the passer should make certain that they are close enough to the blocker to make good contact with their forearm as they start the spin.

Covering Receivers

On any offensive pass play, you will have a group of defensive players rushing the quarterback as he sets up to throw and the remaining defensive players trying to prevent the ball from being caught if it is thrown by the quarterback. These remaining players are involved in what is called the pass coverage. These players usually include the defensive backs and the linebackers. The primary objective in covering receivers is to stop them from catching the pass, and if they do, to make certain that they are tackled immediately. The defense must be able to cover the receivers to stop the offense from moving the ball through the air.

Proper Alignment

In a proper alignment, the defensive corners should line up 5 to 7 yards off the wide receivers. The safeties should line up 8 to 12 yards deep off the tight end or slot receiver. If you are playing only one safety, he should line up deep in the middle of the field. From this position the corners and safeties are in position to make plays if the offense runs or passes the ball.

Backpedal

When an offensive play begins, the defensive backs need to start moving away from the line of scrimmage until they determine whether it is a running or pass play. Running backward—backpedaling—is the initial movement your defensive backs will make at the start of every play. The backpedal should start with a step backward with the back foot and a push off the front foot. As players backpedal, they should bend forward at the waist and reach back with each step and pull the body over their feet. Their arms should move in a normal, relaxed running fashion. They should keep their shoulders in front of their hips. Players should remain under control so that when receivers make their break to their final pattern to catch the ball, the defenders are ready to drive on them.

Coaching Tip

If players have trouble maintaining a smooth backpedal, make sure that they are not leaning back and that their hips and shoulders are not behind their feet.

Pass Coverage

You will consider two basic types of pass coverage as part of your defensive tactics. In man-to-man coverage, one defender is assigned to and stays with one receiver all over the field for the entire offensive play. In zone coverage, the defensive players drop—move into—a designated area of the field and are responsible for deflecting any pass thrown into that area.

Man-to-Man Pass Coverage   In a man-to-man defense, each player on the defense covers a specific offensive player (see figure 7.10). This defense works best when you have athletic players with speed and the ability to run backward and react to the offensive player's pass pattern. Playing man-to-man pass defense requires mental toughness and a willingness to accept the challenge of staying with a receiver for the entire play. You must also consider the team you are playing. If your defenders can match your opponent in speed and athletic ability, you may want to feature a man-to-man pass defense to provide tight coverage on your opponent's pass receivers.

When using the man-to-man pass coverage, defensive players must keep their eyes focused on the belt region of the receiver they are responsible for. They should maintain a 3- to 4-yard cushion between themselves and the receiver and should never turn their back on their receiver. Defensive players should learn to let the receiver take them to the ball by recognizing and reacting to the receiver's pattern. Players should look for the ball only when they are running with the receiver and can physically reach out and touch the receiver.

Zone Pass Coverage   In a zone defense, each defensive player covers a certain area of the field (see figure 7.11). Zone coverage is different from man-to-man coverage; the defensive players are assigned an area of the field to cover, and they focus their eyes on the quarterback, not on a particular receiver as they do in man-to-man pass coverage. Zone pass coverage can help guard against big

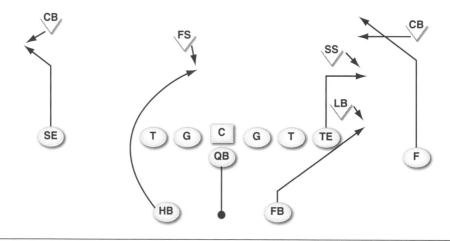

Figure 7.10   Man-to-man pass coverage (5-2 cover 1).

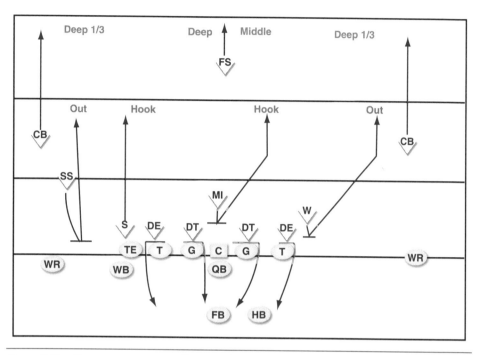

Figure 7.11   Zone pass coverage alignment (4-3 cover 3).

offensive plays because defensive help from another defensive player is never too far away. Mistakes made in zone defenses often are not as costly as those made in man-to-man defenses. This is a good type of pass defense to use when your opponent has superior speed. A disadvantage of the zone defense is that the opponent can overload a zone by putting more offensive receivers into the zones than there are defensive players. In this case, the defender in that zone should cover the deepest offensive player in the zone until the ball is thrown to an offensive receiver in front of him.

When using zone coverage, players line up in their respective positions, and on the snap, players drop into their assigned areas—zones—on the field. Each player should focus on the quarterback and the ball and watch for the ball to leave the quarterback's hand. When the quarterback is set and ready to throw, the underneath defensive players (the defensive players not assigned to cover a deep area of the field) should stop their backpedal, settle, and take short, choppy steps. The players assigned to a deep zone should continue their backpedal in their deep zone until the quarterback releases the ball. As the quarterback starts moving forward to throw, all the defensive players should break in that direction and allow the ball to take them to the intended receiver.

Coaching Tip

Breaking up the pass, either by deflecting the ball away from the receiver or by jarring the ball loose when it is just being caught, is a great defensive play and is equal to tackling the ball carrier on a running play before the ball carrier gains yardage.

Coaching Tip

In a game, if the quarterback is completing passes over the heads of the defensive players in the underneath zones, make sure that these players are not stopping their drop or coming up, reacting to an offensive receiver crossing the field in front of them.

When drilling players on zone pass defense, do not use receivers. Instead, use a cone or a shirt to designate the location of the wide receivers and tight end, and use one player, acting as a quarterback, to drop back a full five steps, set up, step, and pass. This teaches the defensive players to focus on the quarterback and the ball and to break in the direction of the pass the minute the ball leaves the passer's hand.

Once receivers are reintroduced into the drill, you may see that a defensive player is not reacting the instant the quarterback throws the ball. Immediately check to see where the defender is looking. Is he looking at the receiver running in his zone instead of looking at the quarterback?

Three-Deep Zone-Drop Drill

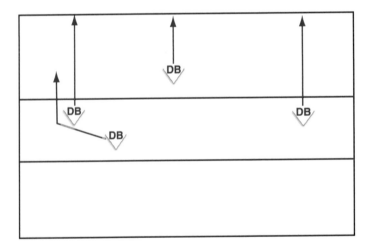

Defensive backs (DB) position themselves as shown in the diagram. The coach designates which DB drops first. Once the DB is in a proper stance, on the coach's command, the DB drops into the proper zone using the backpedal technique. As the DB drops, the focus should be on the coach and the ball. You may practice the strong safety's drop by having the DBs sprint to get width, swing the inside leg around, and then move into the backpedal. After the DB has dropped 7 or 8 yards, the coach can raise the ball, point in the direction of a pass, and then throw the ball. The DB should roll over his foot in that direction and break to the area of the pass. Players drop one at a time and repeat the drill as an entire group. This drill can also be adapted for a two-deep zone by indicating two DBs to act as safeties and aligning them.

Defensive Tactics

Every defense has a purpose. It can be designed to blitz, penetrate, pursue, contain, or perform in various ways to disrupt or stop the offense when they run the ball. You can align the 11 players that make up the defensive team in a variety of ways. This alignment indicates the number of actual players from each defensive group (defensive line, linebackers, and defensive backs) that you have on the field for any play. Your defensive alignment must capitalize on the team's strengths and compensate for its weaknesses. For example, if you have a somewhat big, slow team, use more players on the line of scrimmage and try to control and contain the offense. If you have a small, quick team, use more linebackers and do more blitzing to take advantage of their quickness. Once you have determined your style of defense, stay with it. The following are the three most important goals a defensive team can strive to accomplish:

1. *Prevent the easy touchdown.*

   Although the obvious objective on defense is to keep the opposition from scoring, a more functional objective of defensive play is to prevent the opposition from scoring the easy touchdown with a long pass or a long run. Your opponent must earn every point it scores if you have a defense that challenges every yard. Emphasize to your defense that stopping a team on third down is vital and praise players for preventing third downs that force the offense to give up the ball.

2. *Get possession of the ball.*

   The defensive team may gain possession of the ball by preventing the opponent from gaining the next first down on four downs, forcing a punt, recovering a fumble, or intercepting a pass. Players, especially defensive backs, should be cautioned never to gamble on an interception if missing the ball can result in a touchdown.

3. *Score.*

   The defense can score by returning a punt, a fumble, or an intercepted pass. The defense also can score by downing the ball carrier in the offense's own end zone for a safety.

In addition to these three important goals, you must also be flexible; understand the differences between man-to-man and zone coverages; teach your players attacking, contain, and pressure defenses; and keep your defense fun. Finally, as your players advance, you will teach them how to read the offensive plays.

Flexibility

Team defense involves a group of players performing their individual techniques for the good of the team. Get the right players at the point of attack at the right time, and your team will be successful.

The offense's position on the field, the score, the time left in the game, and the type of offense your team is facing are all factors that influence the defense that you should run. You must prepare the defense to cover various formations and series of plays. For example, if the offense lines up with a wing back and is running the ball successfully to that side, you could slant your entire defensive line into the gaps in that direction. If the offensive team is employing a spread formation using three or four wide receivers, you may want to use a four-deep coverage and substitute an extra defensive back into the game for a linebacker.

By knowing the mechanics of football and learning as much as you can about the strengths and weaknesses of your defense, you will be able to make the proper adjustments during the game. You should also consider limiting the defense according to the skill level of your team. It is more effective to run a few defenses well than to run many defenses poorly.

Defensive Alignments

It is important to take a closer look at the different types of defensive alignments to see how your choice of coverage can affect the game.

Man-to-Man Defense

In man-to-man defense, each player on the defense is assigned a specific offensive player to cover. This defense works best when you have athletic players with speed. Inexperienced or slower players tend to get beat more often in one-on-one situations, leading to big gains or scores for the other team.

Think in terms of the team you are playing. If they have fast, athletic receivers, you may want to play a zone defense to reduce the risk of getting beat for a big play. Consider how your opponents are performing as well as the abilities of your own players when deciding whether or not to use a man-to-man coverage.

Zone Defense

In a zone defense, each defensive player is assigned a certain area of the field to cover. A zone can help guard against big plays; defensive help is never too far away. Mistakes made in zone defenses often are not as costly as those made in man-to-man defenses. A disadvantage of using a zone is that the opponent can overload a zone; in this case the defender in that zone should cover the deepest offensive player in the zone until the ball is thrown to a different player.

By carefully analyzing the abilities of your opponent and your team, you will be better prepared to make a proper decision on whether to use the man-to-man or zone coverage. In addition to knowing how and when to use those coverages, you must know the basics of attacking defense, pressure defense, and contain defense.

Attacking Defense

Use the attacking defense when the offense moves the ball rather well or if your defense is particularly strong. When using the attacking defense, adjust your basic alignment based on what your opponent is doing. For example, if the other team is running the ball up the middle at your linebackers, switch to a defense that puts a defensive line player in the middle who can move across the line of scrimmage, through the gaps—or spaces—between the offensive blockers. The hope is that this will disrupt the blocking of the offensive play and your team can gain the advantage.

Coaching Tip

Incorporate the best physical skills of your defensive players in your defense and then work to perfect these strengths rather than trying to teach every type of defense to your players.

Pressure Defense

A pressure defense uses eight players within 5 yards of the line of scrimmage who can rush or be in position to play the run (see figure 7.12). One or more linebackers are assigned to blitz—charge across the line of scrimmage—through predetermined gaps the instant the ball is snapped. The pressure defense forces the offensive team to make mistakes. An example of this type of pressure is when the defense forces the quarterback to throw the football before he is ready by rushing the linebackers in addition to the defensive linemen at the quarterback as he sets up to throw. The pressure defense also changes the tempo of the game, preventing the opponent from retaining possession of the football and driving down the field.

Use the pressure defense when you are confident in your players' abilities and techniques. This is important because in this defense your defensive backs are isolated one on one with their receivers in true man-to-man coverage and may not get help from the safety.

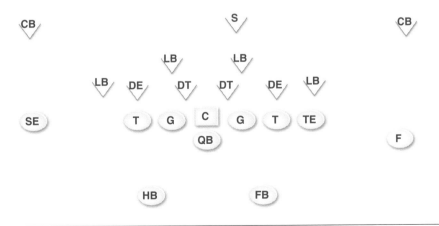

Figure 7.12   Pressure defense alignment (S 4-4 defense).

The pressure defense provides a good change-up, rather than being the defense you use on every down. Have it ready to use in all down-and-distance situations where you need added pressure across the line to stop the offensive team. You may not want your defensive backs playing man-to-man pass coverage for the entire game, but use the pressure defense when you feel that they can execute the pass coverage for a few plays each game without being beaten on a deep pass route. If you find a blitz that gives the offense trouble or that they cannot pick up, keep using it until they make the proper adjustment.

When using pressure defense, teach your defensive players the following points:

- A pressure defense uses man-to-man pass coverage and tries to bump receivers as the receivers start to run their pass routes.
- Designated linebackers attack the line of scrimmage on the snap, trying to disrupt the offensive players' blocking schemes.
- Defensive players can jump up into the line of scrimmage and then retreat. They can loop on their pass rush. They can overpower an offense by rushing more defensive players on one side of the ball than there are offensive players to block.

Contain Defense

The contain defense plays a little softer than the attacking or pressure defense, and its goal is to keep the offense from getting outside or deep. This type of defense requires disciplined players who fully carry out their assignments. It is effective in normal and long-yardage situations just before the half and at the end of the game to ensure a victory. Effective tactical coaching is very important to the success of a contain defense. The defensive players must be able to recognize formations, types of running plays, and types of passes and must adjust to stop the play.

In a contain defense, the defensive player who has contain (the responsibility for turning the ball carrier back to the center of the field), the end man on the line of scrimmage, a defensive end, linebacker, or defensive back who is aligned and in position to be able to react to any blocker and ball carrier who tries to run outside of them. After defensive players read their keys, they first control the gaps or areas of the field that they are responsible for and then react to the football. The defensive backs may use zone coverage on passes to ensure that the receivers do not get behind them. Figure 7.13 shows a sample alignment for a contain defense.

Coaching Tip

When you find that defensive players are late in moving to their assigned gaps, make sure that they are lining up so that they can see the center snap the ball and move with the movement of the ball.

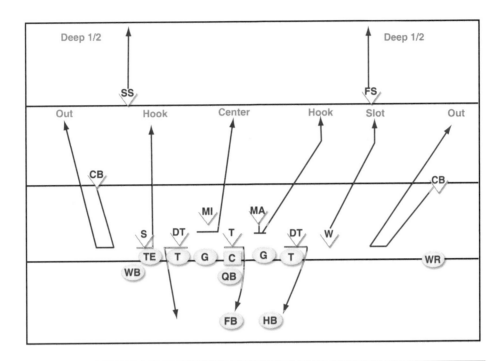

Figure 7.13   Contain defense alignment (3-4 cover 2).

Reading the Play

It is important for every defensive player to have fun, and one way to increase their enjoyment is to teach them how to read offensive plays. This is a more advanced skill, so you should stick to just a few reads and be sure to keep it as simple as possible.

The most basic read is made by "keying" in on an opponent's formation, tendencies in play selection, or individual player cues. For example, the first key for defensive linemen or linebackers is the player directly in front of them, then the offensive player to their right or left. The movement of the player directly in front of the defensive player should alert the defensive player to a run or pass play. If the offensive linebacker or blocking back sets up to pass-protect, the defensive players can assume it's a pass play and focus on covering their receiver. If the defensive players see the linebacker or blocking back drive-block, they can anticipate a running play and move into position to stop the ball carrier.

In addition to paying attention to what the offense is doing, defensive players also need to understand their team's defense for the play, because the type of coverage will affect the decisions they make. For example, with both a zone or man-to-man pass coverage, defensive backs can look in at the quarterback at the start of the play to try to pick up cues that the quarterback is sending. In man-to-man, however, after two steps, the defensive back must refocus on the wide receiver.

8

Coaching Special Teams

All phases of the kicking segments of a football game are referred to as "special teams." Just as you teach the offensive and defensive segments to your team, you also will coach all phases of the kicking game. At times, players focus more on their duties on offense and defense and downplay their roles as special teams players. However, special teams are an integral part of a successful football team, and you, as the coach, must remind all players that their contribution on special teams is just as important as their contribution on offense and defense.

Kicking-Game Rules

The following are special rules that apply only to special teams and should be taught to players as you coach the different phases of the kicking game:

- A player signals a fair catch by extending an arm above the head and waving it from side to side. The receiving player cannot hit or be hit after a fair catch, and the ball cannot be advanced after the catch.
- The kicking team may down the football after the ball has hit the ground.
- No one on either team may block below the waist.
- No player on the receiving team may touch the punter or kicker unless the receiving team has blocked the kick or the kicker runs with the ball.
- A field goal is a scrimmage kick and uses the same rules as the punt.
- On a kickoff, after the ball has traveled 10 yards, it is a free ball and either team can gain possession of it.

In this chapter, we first discuss the technical skills you will teach your team. Then, we focus on the special teams tactics you will use.

Special Teams Technical Skills

The phases of the kicking game can be broken into two general areas. The first is when your team kicks the ball during a kickoff, punt, point after touchdown (PAT), or a field goal. The second area is when your team receives a kick and you try to block a PAT or field goal during a kickoff return or punt return. The kicking game comprises about one-fourth of a football game. This means that as a coach you must plan for and devote part of your practice time each day to one or two phases of the kicking game.

Let's first work to understand the basic technical skills involved with special teams, focusing on the punt team, the kickoff team, the placekicking team, the kickoff and punt return teams, and the PAT and field goal–blocking teams. Then, we move onto the tactics involved with these special teams.

Punt Team

The punt team is the special teams segment used most often during a game because teams almost always punt on fourth down. The punt team consists of two players. The center, known as the long snapper, centers the ball back between the legs to the punter who can be lined up 10 to 15 yards away depending on the ability of the center. The punter catches the snap from the center and executes the punt. The remaining players block the opposing players until the punter kicks the ball. After the punt, they run down the field prepared to tackle opposing players attempting to run the punt back up the field.

Punt coverage involves organizing your punt team so that they can cover the punt and down the ball carrier before he can advance the ball upfield. The punter should kick the ball for distance and keep it in the air long enough to give the coverage team time to get downfield and make the play.

If the punter does not have time to get the ball off, make sure the players know that they must block first, before the ball is kicked and before they make their way down the field.

Long Snapper

When centering to the punter, long snappers start with the feet even and then reach out to grip the ball as though throwing a forward pass with the snapping hand. The other hand rests lightly on top of the ball and guides the ball during the snap. In the stance the shoulders are even and the back level so that the shoulders and rear end are at the same height. When long snappers see that the punter is ready, they snap the ball with both hands back between their legs to the punter with as much force as possible, aiming for the punter's belt. As they snap the ball, they allow the hands to rotate to the outside. The long snapper's most important job is getting the ball to the punter.

If the long snapper throws the ball over the punter's head, make sure the back is level. If the rear end is higher than the shoulders, the snap will be too high. Keeping the back level will lower the snap.

Coaching Tip

Set up a specific time during practice to concentrate as a team on a phase of special teams. During this time, work on corresponding phases of the kicking game. For example, in practice one, focus on the punt and punt return team by practicing the fake punt pass or run-and-punt blocks if used; in practice two, focus on the kickoff and kickoff return teams by practicing onside kicks and onside prevent team; and in practice three, focus on the PAT and field goal team and the field goal block team by practicing fake field goal runs or the pass-and-fake defense.

Punter

Teams punt on fourth down to turn the ball over to the opponent. The punting team's objective is to give the opponent a less favorable field position. Coach your kickers to follow these guidelines for punting successfully:

- Line up 10 yards behind the center.
- When catching the ball, position as shown in figure 8.1a, and once the ball is received, take a short step forward with the kicking foot and extend the ball forward. Then, take a normal second step with the nonkicking foot and allow the hand opposite the kicking foot to come away from the ball.
- When the ball is dropped, there should be no movement at the elbows, wrists, or shoulders, and the ball should drop parallel to the ground with the tip turned slightly in, as shown in figure 8.1b.
- As the kick is made, the nonkicking leg should remain in contact with the ground and the kicking leg should make proper contact on the center of the ball, as shown in figure 8.1c. The kicking leg will then extend and follow through. Also remember that foot speed is not as important as making proper contact with the ball.

Coaching Tip

Remind your players to keep their shoulders in front of their hips during the entire kicking motion.

a   b   c

Figure 8.1   *(a-c)* Proper kicking technique for the punter.

Punting Drill

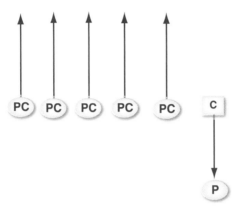

Players divide into two groups. The first group includes the center (C) and the punter (P). The second group includes the punt coverage team (PC). Both groups are positioned as shown in the diagram. The P lines up 10 yards behind the C. When the C sees that the P is ready, the C throws the ball back to the P with as much force as possible, aiming for the belt of the P. When the P receives the ball, the P kicks the ball. When the ball is in the air, the PC team charges downfield so that they can cover the punt. Break up the PC team so that only one side goes at a time (e.g., everyone left of the C, as shown in the diagram, and then everyone to the right of the C). That way, you can rotate players and keep the drill going. You may also add a punt return group to enhance the drill.

The key to coaching punters is to teach correct technique and then allow them to practice and develop their rhythm. They should strive for consistency in height and distance.

Kickoff Team

This is the team that will be on the field after you have scored and at the beginning of the game or the start of the second half. The kicker is the only player on this team who uses a special technique. The remaining 10 players on the kickoff team run down the field as the ball is kicked and try to get into position to tackle the returner, who is trying to run the ball back up the field. Kickoff coverage is configured the same as punt coverage as shown in figure 8.2.

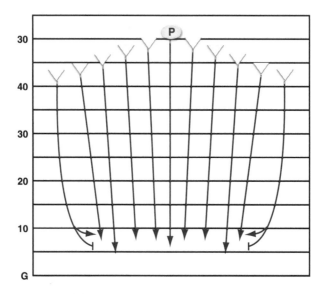

Figure 8.2   Kickoff team alignment.

Kicker

To kick the ball down the field as far as possible, the kicker must run at the ball to build momentum for the kick. To achieve this momentum, the kicker should do the following:

- Place the ball on the tee.
- Line up with the kicking foot directly behind the ball and the tee and place the nonkicking foot to the side of the tee.
- Take one step back with the kicking foot.
- Turn and take approximately eight more steps straight back from the ball.
- Turn and make certain he is still in line with the ball.
- Turn and take five steps to the side opposite the kicking foot.
- Face the ball and take a short step forward with the kicking foot.
- Start the forward run to the ball by taking a short step forward with the kicking foot.
- Slowly build speed and momentum on the approach to the ball.
- Place the nonkicking foot four inches behind and six inches outside the ball, pointing straight down the field.

Coaching Tip

If the kicker is not getting elevation on the ball, the plant foot may be too far away from the ball. This causes the kicking foot to make contact with the ball at the center of the ball or higher, resulting in a low kick.

- Keep the shoulders forward, eyes on the ball, and kicking leg behind the body and allow the kicking leg and foot to swing in a nice arch to the ball.
- Hit the ball with the top of the arch on the kicking foot at a point four inches from the bottom point of the ball.
- Keep the head down throughout the kick and allow the kicking leg to follow though in a smooth motion.
- Become a safety and get in position in front of the path of the returner.

Remainder of the Kickoff Team

The two outside players on the kickoff team should run down near the sideline and make certain that the kickoff returner cannot get to the outside of the field. Emphasize to your players that they should do the following:

- Stay in the same position relative to their teammates as they run down the field.
- Never follow a teammate's path down the field.
- Avoid blockers on the same side the ball is being returned on.
- Maintain control by shortening their stride as they near the ball carrier so that they are in position to make the tackle.

Coaching Tip
If players are missing tackles, remind them to shorten their stride, widen their base, and be prepared to go to the left or right, as they near the ball carrier.

Placekicking Team

This is the phase of the kicking game you'll use when your team attempts to score points by kicking a point after touchdown or kicking a field goal if the drive has been stopped and you are close enough to the opponent's goal line. During this phase of the kicking game, three players use special techniques: the kicker, who makes the kick; the holder, who catches the ball from the center and places it on the tee; and the center—known as the short snapper—who centers the ball back to the holder. The remaining eight players block the opposing players so that the kick can be made.

Kicker

The two basic types of placekicks are the straight-ahead style and soccer style. Both are equally effective. Kickers should follow these steps, regardless of the kicking style they use:

- Stand three steps behind where the ball will be placed (one and a half to two steps to the side for soccer style). The kicking foot should be slightly behind the nonkicking foot, and the eyes should be on the spot where the ball will be placed.

Coaching Tip
If the kicker misses either to the right or the left of the goalposts, make sure that the nonkicking foot is pointed at the middle of the goalposts.

- Take a short step with the nonkicking leg and then a slightly longer-than-normal step with the kicking leg, as shown in figure 8.3a.
- Plant the nonkicking foot about a shoe's length away from the ball, to the side of the ball. This should be pointed at the middle of the goalposts. At the same time, bend the kicking leg behind the body and use a smooth swing (see figure 8.3b).
- Point the toe to create a smooth, hard surface. Contact the ball on the large bone on top of the foot. The point of contact should be about four inches above the lower end of the ball (see figure 8.3c).
- Use a full follow-through. Finish with the leg in line with the opposite shoulder.

a

b

c

Figure 8.3 *(a-c)* Placekicking steps.

Holder

The holder should be able to catch the ball with ease and have the dexterity to place the ball on the tee correctly. Once the kicking tee is placed on the ground 7 yards from the line of scrimmage, the holder should assume the position to receive the snap from the short snapper and do the following:

- Kneel with the back knee on the ground and the front leg up with the foot pointing at the center of the goalpost.
- Reach down with the back hand to make sure the tee is within reach.
- Look to see if the kicker is ready to make the kick.
- Place both little fingers and thumbs together to form the target for the short snapper.
- Catch the snap and guide the ball to the tee with both hands.
- Place the index finger of the back hand on the top point to balance the ball.
- Use the other hand to gently spin the ball to place the laces of the ball to the front.

Coaching Tip
If holders have trouble catching the snap, make sure that their hands are placed properly with the thumbs together and palms facing forward and up and that they can see their hands and the ball as they make the catch.

Short Snapper

When centering to the holder, the short snapper uses the same stance and technique taught to the long snapper (see page 127). The difference is that the distance of the snap is shorter, and the target area—the holder's hands—is lower than the waist-high target of the punter. Once the snap is made, the short snapper should bring the forearms up, ready to help block.

Remainder of the Placekicking Team

The remaining players on the placekicking team always block to their inside gap first when the ball is snapped. Work with your players to focus on the following:

- Step back with the inside foot to gain power.
- Lean to the inside.
- Block whomever comes inside.

Kickoff and Punt Return Team

These two phases of the kicking game come into play when your opponent is either kicking off or punting the ball. The players who use special technique are the players who catch the kick and return it up the field. The other players' major assignment is to block for the return after they are certain that the ball has been kicked.

Kick Return Players

The players who return kicks must be able to catch and be able to run the ball after the catch. The players should line up in position to see the kicker or punter before the snap. For both returns, line up two players on each side of the field. Based on the flight of the ball, one return player calls out to the other, "I have it. I have it." The other player moves up to block. Once the kick is made, kick returners making the catch should do the following:

- Move so that they are in front of the flight of the ball.
- Reach up with both hands, with the little fingers together, so that they can see both the ball and their hands as the ball comes down.
- Bring the ball into the body and secure it as they start the return to the designated area of the field.
- Run the ball as far up the field as possible before being tackled.

Coaching Tip

On the kickoff, if the returner is tackled immediately and cannot return the ball, make sure that the blockers are dropping back and positioning their bodies between the coverage players they are assigned to block and the area designated to the returner to return the kick.

Punt return players have the option of catching the punt, allowing it to hit the ground, and stopping or catching the ball after signaling for a "fair catch" by waving one arm back and forth high above their heads. Players signaling for a fair catch cannot run after the catch, and opposing players cannot tackle them.

Blockers

The remaining players on the kickoff and punt return team should each be assigned a player to block during the kick return. Players should be sure that the ball is kicked and then position themselves between their assigned player and the area (left, middle, or right) where the ball is to be returned.

Players blocking below the waist are usually leaving their feet and diving to make their block. Players should aim for the front numbers on the jersey and run through the block.

Return Drill

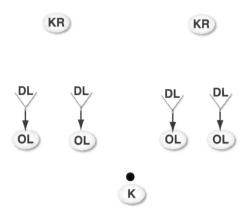

Players divide into two groups. The first group includes the kicker (K) and the rest of the kickoff team on the line (DL). The second group includes the kickoff returners (KR) and the rest of the kickoff return team on the line (OL). Players position themselves as shown in the diagram. The K places the ball on the tee. Half of each group goes each time so that the drill can continue without breaks. The KRs practice calling the ball, making the catch, and using the blocks, while OLs practice making their assigned blocks.

Point After Touchdown (PAT) and Field Goal—Blocking Team

Keep your defensive team on the field whenever your opponent lines up to attempt a PAT or field goal. The opponent can still run or pass the ball, so it's important to stay alert and be sure that the ball is kicked. Players not involved in pass coverage should rush across the line on the snap and try to get their hands up to deflect the kick. Caution players to never touch or run into the kicker on any kick. If your players run into the kicker, remind them that this is a penalty. They can avoid this by focusing on a point 3 yards in front of the kicker and blocking the ball as it leaves the kicker's foot. See figure 8.4 for an example of alignment for specialists on PAT or field goal teams.

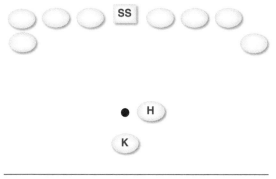

Figure 8.4   Specialist alignment for a PAT or field goal.

Special Teams Tactics

The primary objective of special teams is to execute the basic elements of the kicking game without making big mistakes. Its second objective is to attack an opponent's weakness or exploit a situation when it arises. Special teams require thought and planning before playing games. The major areas of special teams include the following:

- Special teams kicking segments: kickoff and punt, resulting in a change of possession and (you hope) poor field position for your opponent
- Special teams scoring segment: PAT and field goal, resulting in the kicking team scoring points
- Special teams returning segments: kickoff and punt return, resulting in possession of the ball and gaining as much positive yardage as possible on the return
- Special teams kick-blocking segment: PAT and field goal blocking, resulting in stopping the opponent from scoring by a kick

Special teams require not only special skills from some of your players, but they also require you to carefully plan when you will use each segment in a game. Well before the game begins, you must consider all the potential situations that could require the kicking game, paying special attention to how you might substitute on special teams in the case of injury. We first focus on goals that you can implement with your special teams then we discuss these four major areas of special teams to help you better understand the tactics involved.

Kicking Segment

If you are not receiving the kick, you use your kickoff team at the start of the game or the beginning of the third quarter. You also use the kickoff team after you score a touchdown or field goal. Players on the kickoff team should be fast and be good tacklers. One member must be able to kick the ball off a tee. The ball on a kickoff is called a "live ball," and either team can recover and gain possession after the kick.

You normally use your punt team on fourth down, when your offense has failed to gain the necessary 10 yards for a first down. When punting from their own end of the field, teams typically punt from a tight formation with both outside players lined up close to the next outside player on the line of scrimmage in order to prevent the opposing team from blocking the punt. When you are at your opponent's end of the field, be ready to decide what to do on fourth down. You can punt the ball, try for a field goal, or run an offensive play and try to gain the yardage needed for a first down. Anticipate what you must do so that you can make the decision without hesitation or calling a timeout. Players on your punt team should be able to first block for the punter and then tackle the opposing player returning the punt. Two

Goals for Special Teams

You can help your special teams be successful by setting goals for them and by developing a successful strategy. The location on the field where the offense starts each drive—the first play of a new series—is often governed by the execution of your special teams. This starting location—field position—is important to your team's success. The main goal of the special teams is to help the team win. Penalties must be avoided. Your special teams players must understand that getting possession of the ball and returning the ball as far as possible up the field are important goals for all return teams. Finally, the teams kicking the ball—coverage teams—must understand that limiting return yardage gained by all kick return teams is equally important. When dealing with special teams, consider the following general rules:

- Know and adhere to the seven "dos" of special teams in order to reach team goals. These are:
  1. Stay onside, and watch the ball.
  2. Avoid running into the kicker. Aim for a spot 1 yard in front of the punter's final leg swing and take the ball off his foot when blocking the punt.
  3. Focus on blocking players from the front on all returns. If the number on the back of the jersey is visible, avoid the block.
  4. Keep blocks above the waist.
  5. Try to play error-free football, especially in the kicking game.
  6. Eliminate penalties that give the ball back to the offense or give them good field position.
  7. Win the battle of field position (on a kickoff, keep the opponents inside their 30-yard line). Good kicking and good coverage will accomplish this.

- Be aware of the following skills that are important to the success of special teams:
  - Make it a priority to eliminate bad snaps. Plan extra practice time for your short snapper, holder, and placekicker to work together on your PAT and field goal team and for your long snapper and punter to work as a unit on the punt team.
  - The punt and kickoff coverage teams must make sure that the ball is kicked before they cover.
  - Anytime there is a kick, the return team must avoid being the victim of a fake play by making sure that the other team has actually kicked the ball into the air.
  - Alert your team to any big plays on special teams (e.g., onside kicks, turnovers, blocked kicks, and fake punts and field goals).

players need specialized skills: The center must be able to snap the ball back to the punter, and the punter must be able to punt the ball. The members of the punting team can down the punt, stopping the return but cannot gain possession of the ball unless a member of the opposition touches the ball.

Scoring Segment

After scoring a touchdown, the scoring team has the opportunity to score an additional point after touchdown, or PAT, by running, passing, or kicking the ball from a tee through the uprights and over the crossbar of the goalpost. Because of the difficulty in finding young players who can kick an extra point, many teams run or pass for this score. If you can develop a player with strong kicking skills, you can easily score by kicking a PAT, and you also have the potential to score three points by kicking a field goal on fourth down.

As a coach, you must know how far your kicker can kick the ball so that you can make the decision to try a field goal if the situation arises in the game. Kicking a PAT or field goal requires three players with special skills: the center to snap the ball to the holder; the holder, who catches the snap and places the ball on the tee; and the kicker. The remaining players on the team must be good blockers to ensure that the kicker has time to make the kick.

Kick-Returning Segment

Your kickoff return team will be on the field anytime your opponent lines up for a kickoff. Before the kickoff return team takes the field, you must tell them where you want the ball returned to, usually to the right, middle, or left side of the field. Typically, two players who can catch the kickoff and run with the ball line up deep down the field. During pregame warm-ups, try to determine how far the opposing kicker can kick off so that you can position your returners at the proper depth. After one of the returners calls the ball, the other becomes a blocker. The remaining nine players on your kickoff return team should have good balance and be able to run and block opposing players as they run down the field. Remind every player on the kickoff return team that a kickoff is a "live ball" and that they must recover and gain possession of the ball if it is kicked to them.

Your punt return team needs to be on the field anytime your opponent lines up to punt the ball. As with a kickoff return, line up two players deep down the field who have the ability to catch the punt and the skill to run with the ball. During the pregame warm-up, try to determine the distance the opposing punter will punt the ball so that you can position the two returners at the proper depth. The remaining nine players on the punt return team must be sure that the punter actually punts the ball and then be able to run and block opposing players as they run down the field. Players should remember that once the ball is punted, your team has possession of it and every punt does not have to be caught or recovered. The players waiting to return the punt can catch the punt and return it up the field, signal and make a fair catch and take possession of the ball at the spot of the catch, or let the ball hit the ground and roll until it is downed by an opposing player or the official blows his whistle to signal that the play has ended. Every player on the punt return team must remember that the opponent does not have to punt the ball, they may try to run or pass for a first down from punt formation.

Kick-Blocking Segment

Anytime an opponent lines up to kick a PAT or field goal you should have a group of 11 players on the field to try to block the kick if this is allowed by your league. Players on the block team who rush the kicker must have the quickness and the desire to block the kick. Rush players on the block team should rush through the gaps between blockers and then raise their arms to deflect the kick. Remind every player on the PAT and field goal block team that the opponent does not have to kick the ball; instead they may try to run or pass for a first down from the PAT and field goal formation. Assign players not rushing to block the PAT or field goal coverage on eligible receivers in case the opponent tries to fake the kick and pass the ball. Caution every rush player on the block team to avoid running into the kicker. This is a penalty that usually results in the opponent getting a first down.

Coaching on
Game Day

Contests provide the opportunity for your players to show what they've learned in practice. Just as your players' focus shifts on contest days from learning and practicing to competing, your focus shifts from teaching skills to coaching players as they perform those skills in contests. Of course, the contest is a teaching opportunity as well, but the focus is on performing what has been learned, participating, and having fun.

In previous chapters you learned how to teach your players techniques and tactics; in this chapter you learn how to coach your players as they execute those techniques and tactics in contests. We provide important coaching principles that will guide you before, during, and after the game.

Before the Contest

Just as you need a practice plan for what you will cover at each practice, you also need a "game plan" for game day. Your written game plan should consist of your best running and passing plays, and the plays you will call on third and one and downs near the opponent's goal line. List the defenses you will use during the game including the number of linemen, linebackers, and defensive backs you will use and the pass coverages and blitzes you have practiced. Also include your defensive call for third and one and your goal line defense. Finally, the game plan should include your method of substitution—alternating players—and the plays that you plan to use during any phase of the kicking game.

Although the game plan is important, you cannot focus on it only on game day. Many coaches focus on how they will coach only during the actual contest, when instead preparations should begin well before the first play of the game. Let's take a closer look at how you can prepare for game-day coaching.

Coaching Tip

Every staff member should be assigned a game-day responsibility and work as one team during the game. While one member of the coaching staff calls all the offensive plays, another staff member can record the plays and the results, while another watches the opponent's defense to detect weaknesses that can be exploited. The same is true when the defense or special teams are on the field.

Coaching Assignments

Game-day preparation should begin in the preseason when, as a staff, you decide and agree on the game-day responsibilities each coach will assume. The staff should decide who will call the offensive and defensive plays, who will handle the special teams, who will substitute, and who will record the calls. As coaches arrive at the game, each staff member should know his or her game-day responsibilities and prepare for the game just as the players do.

Preparations at Practice

A day or two before a contest, you should cover two things—in addition to techniques and tactics—to prepare your players for the game. First, you must decide on specific team tactics you want to use, and second, discuss pregame particulars such as what to eat before the game, what to wear, and when to be at the field. It is also a good idea to walk through the steps for how the team will take the field and where the players will line up on the field for the warm-up and to review the group and team drills that will be used during the warm-up.

Deciding Team Tactics

Some coaches see themselves as great military strategists guiding their young warriors to victory on the battlefield. These coaches burn the midnight oil as they devise complex plans of attack. Team tactics at this level, however, don't need to be complex. The focus should be on consistent execution, moving the ball on offense, and stopping long gains on defense. You should emphasize the importance of teamwork, the responsibility of every player fulfilling their role, and the importance of every player knowing their assignments on offensive plays and defensive alignments. As you become more familiar with your team's tendencies and abilities, you can help them focus on specific tactics that will help them play better.

During the week, inform players of the tactics that you think will work and that you plan to use in the game. Pick out the five running plays, the three pass plays, and the four defenses that you think will have the greatest chance for success in the game. Try to practice this group of plays every practice and make certain that every player understands the plays and that they can run them without error. Limiting the number of plays allows you to repeat them during practice and instill in your players the confidence that they can execute the plays that will be called during the game.

Based on the experience and knowledge of your players, you may want to let them help you determine the first offensive play and first defense that you will call in the game. It is the coach's role to help youngsters grow through the sport experience. Allowing athlete input helps your players learn the game, involves them at a planning level often reserved solely for the coach, and gives them a feeling of ownership. Rather than just "carrying out orders" for the coach, they're executing the plan of attack that they helped decide. Youngsters who have a say in how they approach a task often respond with more enthusiasm and motivation.

Discussing Pregame Particulars

Players need to know what to do before a contest: what they should eat on game day and when, what clothing they should wear to the game, what equipment they should bring, and what time they should arrive at the field.

Discuss these particulars with them at the last practice before a contest. Here are guidelines for discussing these issues.

Pregame Meal   In general, the goal of the pregame meal is to fuel the athlete for the upcoming event, to maximize carbohydrate stores, and to provide energy to the brain. Some foods digest more quickly than others, such as carbohydrate and protein, so we suggest that the athlete consume these rather than fat, which digests more slowly. Good carbohydrate foods include spaghetti, rice, and bran. Good protein foods include low-fat yogurt and boneless, skinless chicken. Athletes should eat foods that they are familiar with and that they can digest easily. Big meals should be eaten three to four hours before the contest. Of course, athletes who don't have time for a pregame meal can use sport beverages and replacement meals, although they are not a good replacement for the pregame meal.

Clothing and Equipment   At the game players need their team uniform, helmet, mouth guard, shoulder pads, girdle pads, thigh pads, knee pads, and shoes. They should wear their pants (with pads) and shoes and carry their remaining equipment to the field and put it on there.

Time to Arrive   Your players need to adequately warm up before a game, so instruct them to arrive 45 minutes before game time to go through the team warm-up (see "Warm-Up" on page 146). You can designate where you want the team to gather as they arrive at the field. Consider making a team rule stating that players must show up 45 minutes before a game and go through the complete team warm-up, or they won't start.

Facilities, Equipment, and Support Personnel

Although the site coordinator and officials have formal responsibilities for facilities and equipment, you should know what to look for to ensure that the contest is safe for all athletes (see "Facilities and Equipment Checklist" in appendix A on page 168).

You should arrive at the field 50 minutes before game time so you can check the field, check in with the site coordinator and officials, and greet your players as they arrive to warm up. If the officials don't arrive before the game when they're supposed to, inform the site coordinator.

Unplanned Events

Part of being prepared to coach is to expect the unexpected. What do you do if players are late? What if you have an emergency and can't make the game or will be late? What if the contest is rained out or otherwise postponed? Being prepared to handle out-of-the-ordinary circumstances will help you if unplanned events happen.

If players are late, you may have to adjust your starting lineup. Although this may not be a major inconvenience, stress to your players the importance of being on time for two reasons:

1. Part of being a member of a team is being committed to and responsible for the other members. When players don't show up, or show up late, they break that commitment.

2. Players need to go through a warm-up to physically prepare for the contest. Skipping the warm-up risks injury.

Communicating With Parents

The groundwork for your communication with parents will have been laid in the parent orientation meeting, through which parents learned the best ways to support their kids'—and the whole team's—efforts on the field. Help parents judge success based not just on the contest outcome, but also on how the kids are improving their performances.

If parents yell at the kids for mistakes made during the game, make disparaging remarks about the officials or opponents, or shout instructions for which tactics to use, ask them to refrain and to instead support the team through their comments and actions. These standards of conduct should all be covered in the preseason parent orientation.

When time permits, as parents gather at the field before a contest and before the team has taken the field, you can let them know in a general sense what the team has been focusing on during the past week and what your goals are for the game. However, your players must come first during this time, so focus on your players during the pregame warm-up.

After a contest, quickly come together as a staff and decide what to say to the team and then informally assess with parents, as the opportunity arises, how the team did based not on the outcome, but on meeting performance goals and playing to the best of their abilities. Help parents see the contest as a process, not solely as a test that is pass/fail or win/lose. Encourage parents to reinforce that concept at home.

An emergency might cause you to be late or miss a game. In these cases, notify your assistant coach, if you have one, or the league coordinator. If notified in advance, a parent of a player or another volunteer might be able to step in for the contest.

Sometimes a game will be postponed because of inclement weather or for other reasons such as unsafe field conditions. If the postponement takes place before game day, you must call every member of your team to let them know. If it happens while the teams are on the field preparing for the game, gather your team members and tell them the news and explain why the game has been postponed. Make sure that all your players have a ride home before you leave—you should be the last to leave.

Warm-Up

Players need to both physically and mentally prepare for a game once they arrive at the field. Physical preparation involves warming up. Conduct the warm-up similarly to practice warm-ups, focusing on practicing skills and stretching. Making sure your players are properly warmed up before the game can help reduce the potential for injury during the contest.

Develop the warm-up so that players practice techniques and tactics that will occur in the game such as blocking, running, or passing the football, receiving the ball, kicking the ball, tackling, and covering receivers. You should also include the drills you use in your daily warm-up, but this doesn't mean that extensive time must be spent on each skill. Limit your repetitions and then finish your warm-up period by having your offensive team run plays against the defensive team with little or no contact. Keep your warm-up sharp by running drills and plays quickly and keeping your players moving. Take time during the warm-up period to individually ask players questions about their assignments and review with them the focus of the game plan.

During the warm-up, remind your players of the following:

- The techniques and tactics that they've been working on in recent practices, focusing on the things they've been doing well and their strengths
- The team tactics you focused on in the previous practice in preparation for this game
- Performing the tactics and skills to the best of their individual abilities and playing together as a team
- Playing hard, smart, and having fun

During the Contest

Throughout the contest, you must keep the game in the proper perspective and help your players do the same. You will observe how your players execute tactics and skills and how well they play together. You will make tactical decisions in several areas. You will model appropriate behavior on the sideline, showing respect for opponents and officials, and will demand the same of your athletes. You will watch out for your athletes' physical safety and psychological welfare in terms of building their self-esteem and helping them manage stress and anxiety. Let's first focus on how you can help your team keep the proper perspective and then we can focus on the tactical decisions for game-day performance.

Proper Perspective

Winning games is the short-term goal of your football program; helping your players learn the tactics, skills, and rules of football and how to become fit and how to be good sports in football and in life are the long-term goals. Your young athletes are "winning" when they are becoming better human beings through their participation in football. Keep that perspective in mind when you coach. You have the privilege of setting the tone for how your team approaches the game. Keep winning and all aspects of competition in proper perspective, and your young players will likely follow suit.

Tactical Decisions

Although you aren't called upon to be a great military strategist, as mentioned before, you are called upon to make tactical decisions in several areas throughout a contest. You'll make decisions about who starts the game and when to enter substitutes, about making slight adjustments to your team's tactics, and about correcting players' performance errors or leaving the corrections for the next practice.

Advanced discussions and decisions by the staff can aid in tactical decisions during a game. One coach should be responsible for calling the offensive plays, one coach for the defensive plays, and one coach for making special teams decisions. In all of these areas, the head coach should be able to add input. On small staffs, individual coaches may have to assume responsibility for more than one area.

> **Coaching Tip**
> During the game when a particular segment of the team is on the field, the focus should be on what is happening on the field and how to prepare for the next call.

Starting and Substituting Players

When considering playing time, make sure that everyone on the team gets to play at least half of each game or adjust your playing time, as necessary, based on league rules. This should be your guiding principle as you consider starting and substitution patterns. We suggest you consider two options in substituting players:

1. *Substituting individually.*

   Replace one player with another. This offers you a lot of latitude in deciding who goes in when, and it gives you the greatest combination of players throughout the game. It can be hard to keep track of playing time, but this could be made easier by assigning an assistant or a parent this task. Be aware of the exact number of plays that your league's rules require each player to play.

   You have the option of substituting players by series when you decide to use individual substitution. You may tell players before the game that they will play two offensive series and then the substitute will play the next two series. Players will then know in advance when they should be on the field.

2. *Substituting by quarters.*

   The advantage of substituting players after each quarter is that you can easily track playing time and players know how long they will be in before they might be replaced. When substituting by quarters, it is still important to keep track of the actual number of plays that each player is on the field.

Adjusting Team Tactics

At the 8-to-9 and 10-to-11 age levels, you probably won't adjust your team tactics significantly during a game. Rather, you'll focus on the basic tactics, and during breaks in the game, you'll emphasize the specific tactics your team needs to work on. However, coaches of 12- to 14-year-olds might have reason to make tactical adjustments to improve their team's chances of performing well and winning. As the game progresses, assess your opponent's style of play and tactics and make adjustments that are appropriate—that is, those that your players are prepared for. You may want to consider the following examples when adjusting team tactics:

- Does your opponent have slow or less skilled defensive backs? If so, you might want to emphasize your passing game.

- Does your opponent have skilled running backs that could break open long runs? If so, you might want to shift your defensive alignment to put more players on the line.

- Does your opponent always run on first down? If so, you might want to stack the line against them on first downs.

- Does the opposing quarterback tend to make poor decisions and rush passes when under pressure? If so, you might want to put more of a rush on the quarterback to try to create turnovers.

Coaching Tip

Have someone record every offensive and defensive call and the result of the play. Then, when that segment of the team is off the field, review the call sheet, noting successful plays and defenses and repeating them until the opponent makes adjustments.

Knowing the answers to these questions can help you formulate a game plan and make adjustments during a game. However, don't stress tactics too much during a game. Doing so can take the fun out of the game for the players. If you don't trust your memory, carry a pen and pad to note which team tactics and individual skills need attention in the next practice.

Correcting Errors

In chapter 5 you learned about two types of errors: learning errors and performance errors. Learning errors are those that occur because athletes don't know how to perform a skill. Performance errors are made not because athletes don't know how to execute the skill, but because they make mistakes in carrying out what they do know.

Sometimes it's not easy to tell which type of error athletes are making. Knowing your athletes' capabilities helps you to determine if they know the skill and are simply making mistakes in executing it or if they don't know how to perform it. If they are making learning errors—that is, they don't know how to perform the skills—note this and cover it at the next practice. Game time is not the time to teach skills.

If they are making performance errors, however, you can help players correct them during a game. Players who make performance errors often do so because they have a lapse in concentration or motivation, or they are simply demonstrating human error. Competition and contact can also adversely affect a young player's technique and a word of encouragement about concentration may help. If you do correct a performance error during a contest, do so in a quiet, controlled, and positive tone of voice during a break or when the player is on the sideline with you.

For those making performance errors, you must determine if the error is just an occasional error that anyone can make or if it is an expected error for a youngster at that stage of development. If the latter is the case, then the player may appreciate your not commenting on the mistake. The player knows it was a mistake and may already know how to correct it. On the other hand, perhaps an encouraging word and a "coaching cue" (such as "remember to follow through on your passes") may be just what the athlete needs. Knowing the players and what to say is very much a part of the "art" of coaching.

> **Coaching Tip**
> Designate an area on the sideline where players gather after coming off the field. In this area, you can speak to them either individually or as a group and make necessary adjustments.

Coach and Player Behavior

Another aspect of coaching on game day is managing behavior—both yours and your athletes'. The two are closely connected.

Coach Conduct

You very much influence your players' behavior before, during, and after a contest. If you're up, your players are more likely to be up. If you're anxious, they'll take notice, and the anxiety can become contagious. If you're negative, they'll respond with worry. If you're positive, they'll play with more enjoyment. If you're constantly yelling instructions or commenting on mistakes and errors, it will be difficult for players to concentrate. Instead, let players get into the flow of the game.

The focus should be on positive competition and on having fun. A coach who overorganizes everything and dominates a game from the sideline is definitely not making the contest fun. So how should you conduct yourself on the sideline? Here are a few pointers:

- Be calm, in control, and supportive of your players.
- Encourage players often, but instruct during play sparingly. Players should focus on their performance during a game, not on instructions shouted from the sidelines.
- If you need to instruct a player, do so when you're both on the sidelines, in an unobtrusive manner. Never yell at players for making mistakes. Instead, briefly demonstrate or remind them of the correct technique and encourage them. Tell them how to correct the problem on the field.

You should also make certain that you have discussed sideline demeanor as a staff and that every coach is in agreement to the way they will conduct themselves on the sideline and then work to stick to it. Remember, you're not playing in the Super Bowl! In this program, football competitions are designed to help players develop their skills and themselves—and to have fun. So coach in a manner at games that helps your players do those things.

Player Conduct

You're responsible for keeping your players under control. Do so by setting a good example and by disciplining when necessary. Set team rules for good behavior. If players attempt to cheat, fight, argue, badger, yell disparaging remarks, and the like, it is your responsibility to correct the misbehavior. Initially, it may mean removing players immediately from the game, letting them calm down, and then speaking to them quietly, explaining that their behavior is not acceptable for your team and if they want to play, they must not repeat the action.

Consider team rules in these areas of game conduct:

- Player language
- Player behavior
- Interactions with officials
- Discipline for misbehavior
- Dress code for competitions

Physical Safety

Chapter 4 is devoted to player safety, but it's worth noting here that safety during contests can be affected by how officials call the rules. If officials aren't calling rules correctly and this risks injury to your players, you must intervene. Voice your concern in a respectful manner and in a way that places the emphasis where it should be: on the athletes' safety. One of the officials' main responsibilities is to provide for athletes' safety. Both you and the officials are working together to protect the players whenever possible. Don't hesitate to address an issue of safety with an official when the need arises.

Player Welfare

All athletes are not the same. Some attach their self-worth to winning and losing. This idea is fueled by coaches, parents, peers, and society, who place great emphasis on winning. Players become anxious when they're uncertain whether they can meet the expectations of others or of themselves—especially when meeting a particular expectation is important to them.

If you place too much importance on the game or cause your athletes to doubt their abilities, they will become anxious about the outcome and their performance. If your players look uptight and anxious during a contest, find ways to reduce both the uncertainties about how their performance will be evaluated and the importance they are attaching to the game. Help athletes focus on realistic personal goals—goals that are reachable and measurable and that will help them improve their performance all while having fun as they play. Another way to reduce anxiety on game day is to stay away from emotional pregame pep talks. Instead remind players of the tactics and plays they will use and to play hard, to do their best, and to have fun.

When coaching during contests, remember that the most important outcome from playing football is to build or enhance players' self-worth. Keep that firmly in mind, and strive to promote this through every coaching decision.

Opponents and Officials

Respect opponents and officials. Without them, there wouldn't be a competition. Officials help provide a fair and safe experience for athletes and, as appropriate, help them learn the game. Opponents provide opportunities for your team to test itself, improve, and excel.

You and your team should show respect for opponents by giving your best efforts. Showing respect means being civil to your opponents. Don't allow your players to "trash talk" or taunt an opponent. This behavior is disrespectful to the spirit of the competition and to the opponent. Immediately remove players from a contest if they disobey your orders in this area.

Remember that officials at this level are quite often teenagers—in many cases they may not be much older than the players themselves—and the level of officiating should be commensurate to the level of play. In other words, don't expect perfection from officials any more than you do from your own players. Especially at younger levels, officials may not make every call, because to do so would stop the contest every 10 seconds. You

> **Coaching Tip**
> Keep your demeanor even and positive on the sidelines, conduct your game responsibility the same regardless of the score, help correct your players' errors in a positive manner, and continue to offer encouragement to each player.

may find that the officials for the younger players only call the most flagrant penalties, those directly affecting the outcome of the game. As long as the calls are being made consistently on both sides and the flagrant penalties are being addressed, most of your officiating concerns will be alleviated.

After the Contest

When the game is over, join your team in congratulating the coaches and players of the opposing team, then be sure to thank the officials. Check on any injuries players sustained during the game and inform players of how to care for them. Be prepared to speak with the officials about any problems that occurred during the game. Then, hold a brief meeting—or "team circle," which is explained later—to ensure that your players are on an even keel, whether they won or lost.

Reactions Following the Game

When celebrating a victory, make sure your team does so in a way that doesn't show disrespect for the opponents. It is okay and appropriate to be happy and celebrate a win, but do not allow your players to taunt the opponents or boast about their victory. Keep winning in perspective. Winning and losing are a part of life, not just a part of sport. If players can handle both equally well, they'll be successful in whatever they do.

Athletes are competitors, and competitors are disappointed in defeat. If your team has made a winning effort, let them know this. After a loss, help them keep their chins up and maintain a positive attitude that will carry over into the next practice and contest.

Coaching Tip

Immediately following a game, regardless of the outcome, stay positive. When the players return to the practice field after a game, make certain that you let the previous game go, make needed corrections, and focus on the next opponent and next game.

Postgame Team Meeting

Following the game, gather your team for a "team circle" in a designated area for a short meeting. The players can sit on the ground or kneel on one knee and they may take off helmets and shoulder pads. Before this meeting, decide as a coaching staff what to say and who will say it. Be sure that the coaching staff speaks with one voice following the game.

If your players have performed well in a game, compliment them and congratulate them. Tell them specifically what they did well, whether they won or lost. This will reinforce their desire to repeat their good performances. Don't use this time to criticize individual players for poor performances in front of teammates. Help players improve their skills, but do so in the next practice, not immediately after a game.

The postgame team circle isn't the time to go over tactical problems and adjustments. The players are either so happy after a win or so dejected after a loss that they won't absorb much tactical information. Your first concern should be your players' attitudes and mental well-being. You don't want them to be too high after a win or too low after a loss. This is the time you can be most influential in keeping the outcome in perspective and keeping them on an even keel. Remember, too, that although the final outcome of the game may be extremely important to you, the staff, and some of the parents, for young players the biggest concern may be whether they will get pizza or not. Realize that the majority of your players are playing the game to have fun, and understand that their desire to go out together for something to eat rather than reliving the game is not a reflection on their desire to play well. Stay positive, allow the players to be kids, and avoid making too much over the outcome of the game.

Finally, make sure your players have transportation home. Be the last one to leave to ensure full supervision of your players.

Developing Season and Practice Plans

We hope you have learned a lot from this book: what your responsibilities are as a coach, how to communicate well and provide for safety, how to teach and shape skills, and how to coach on game days. But game days make up only a portion of your season—you and your players will spend more time in practice than in competition. How well you conduct practices and prepare your players for competition will greatly affect not only your players' enjoyment and success throughout the season, but also your own.

Do Your Research

During the football season, coaches must organize certain practices differently based on the following factors:

- Time of year
- Equipment available
- Weather and field conditions
- Injuries to players

When planning practices, you will divide them into preseason practices with and without pads and regular season practices, depending on the time of year. You will vary both your preseason practices and your practices in season depending on whether or not they fall before scrimmages or games. Later in the chapter, we look closely at practice plans and provide examples you can use during the various times of the year.

While you are developing your season plans before the start of the season, be sure to inventory practice equipment and look over the fields you will use for your practice sessions. Remember that equipment may vary from practice facility to facility. For example, your practice field may be unmarked, so you will need to provide a tape or cones to mark the line of scrimmage and the boundaries of the field. Or, you might lack goalposts on your practice field for your placekicker, but you can still hold kicking practice. Handheld lightweight blocking dummies that are easily transported from practice to practice are useful. Make sure to include in your individual practice plans whatever equipment you will need for each practice.

Regardless of the time of year, be aware of the weather conditions that could force you to shorten or even eliminate a practice session. This is especially true in the preseason when heat might force you to adjust the length of your practice session. In this case, shorten each segment of your practice schedule, include more water breaks, and make sure that your players are not overheating. Also it is important to be aware of lightning during severe weather. If lightning is nearby when the players are on the field, quickly get them to shelter.

Because injuries are unpredictable, you cannot plan for them. But they will occur, and you may need to make on-the-field changes to your practice plan when certain players are unavailable because of injury or sickness. At these times, be flexible and understanding. Have a plan for adjusting your practices under these varying conditions that will allow you to accomplish the most and prevent avoidable injuries.

Season Plans

Before the first practice with your players, sit down as a staff and write down each practice and game date on a calendar. Then go back and number your practices. Those practice numbers will become the foundation of your season plan. Now you can work through the season plan, moving from practice to practice to create a quick overview of what you hope to cover in each practice.

To create a season plan, simply list the practice number, the purpose of the practice, the main skills you will cover, and the drills you will use during the practice. While developing this plan, keep in mind the research that you gathered earlier. Also keep in mind the various skills that your athletes must learn and be sure to cover those skills in your season plan (see chapters 6, 7, and 8 for descriptions of basic skills). Your season plan provides a snapshot of the entire season. See "Sample Season Plan" for an idea of what this overview looks like.

Coaching Tip
Many players have a dream position that they would like to play. The early preseason is the time to let them find out if they have the skills to play the position and how they compare to their teammates.

Sample Season Plan

This plan provides a glimpse of a season plan for 8- to 14-year-olds. It takes a quick look at the first 10 practices in the season. It lists the practice number, the purpose, the main skills to be taught, and the drills to be used. More detailed practice information is listed in the practice plans.

Practice 1 (no pads and noncontact)

Purpose

This practice gives every player a chance to try out for any position and helps you find the players on the team who have the best natural skills required to play specific positions.

Technical Skills and Tactics

Throwing (page 88), punting (page 128), receiving (page 91), and kickoff (page 129)

(continued)

(continued)

Drills

Open throwing drill, open punting drill, open receiving drill, open kickoff drill, and interception drill

Practice 2 (no pads and noncontact)

Purpose

This is a continuation of the first practice. Give every player a chance to try out for any position and find the players who have the best natural skills required to play specific positions.

Technical Skills and Tactics

Throwing (page 88), punting (page 128), receiving (page 91), and kickoff (page 129)

Drills

Open throwing drill, open punting drill, open receiving drill, open kickoff drill, and interception drill

Practice 3 (no pads and noncontact)

Purpose

Begin assigning positions to players and teach them basic defensive, offensive, and special teams concepts. Drills are performed on air and without contact.

Technical Skills and Tactics

Offensive stance (page 62), throwing (page 88), receiving (page 91), drive block (page 68), angle block (page 71), defensive stance (page 104), backpedal (page 115), and kickoff (page 129)

Drills

Open throwing drill, open receiving drill, and punting drill (page 129)

Practice 4 (no pads and noncontact)

Purpose

Continue refining the positions of the players and their alignments. Begin to run basic offensive plays and defenses and special teams plays.

Technical Skills and Tactics

Pass tree (page 100), man-to-man defense (page 116), zone defense (page 116), and punt return (page 133)

Drills

Pass protection–blocking drill (page 81), drop-back drill (page 91), pass rush drill (page 114), and punting drill (page 129)

Practice 5 (no pads and noncontact)

Purpose

This is a continuation of practice 4.

Technical Skills and Tactics
Pass tree (page 100), man-to-man defense (page 116), zone defense (page 116), and punt return (page 133)

Drills
Pass protection–blocking drill (page 81), drop-back drill (page 91), pass rush drill (page 114), and punting drill (page 129)

Practice 6 (pads)

Purpose
Begin working players against one another and introduce the idea of contact on a limited basis.

Technical Skills and Tactics
Tackling (page 108), cross block (page 72), double-team block (page 74), receiving (page 91), and pass tree (page 100)

Drills
Breaking- and receiving-points drill (page 92), cross-blocking drill (page 74), and double team–blocking drill (page 75)

Practice 7 (pads)

Purpose
Building on practice 6, continue helping players become comfortable with contact and begin developing the competition between offense and defense.

Technical Skills and Tactics
Head-on tackling (page 108), angle tackling (page 110), zone blocking (page 75), pass tree (page 100), pass protection (page 78), and pass rush (page 112)

Drills
Head on–tackling drill (page 109), angle-tackling drill (page 111), zone-blocking drill (page 77), drop-back drill (page 91), pass protection–blocking drill (page 81), and pass rush drill (page 114)

Practice 8 (pads)

Purpose
This is a continuation of practices 6 and 7.

Technical Skills and Tactics
Head-on tackling (page 108), angle tackling (page 110), zone blocking (page 75), pass tree (page 100), pass protection (page 78), and pass rush (page 112)

Drills
Head on–tackling drill (page 109), angle-tackling drill (page 111), zone-blocking drill (page 77), drop-back drill (page 91), pass protection–blocking drill (page 81), and pass rush drill (page 114)

(continued)

(continued)

Practice 9 (pads)

Purpose
This practice prepares the team for tomorrow's scrimmage.

Technical Skills and Tactics
To be determined based on where the team is at this point

Drills
To be determined based on where the team is at this point

Practice 10

Purpose
Hold a scrimmage that simulates a real-game experience. Substitute all players according to a substitution plan dedicated to giving all players equal playing time.

Technical Skills and Tactics
All skills could come into play.

Drills
Not applicable

Use your season plan to begin developing individual practices. You may need to adjust your season plan throughout the season, and that is okay. It is meant to serve as a guide that can be revised and adjusted if you and the staff believe the team needs extra work in certain areas or if injuries or equipment issues force you to change your plans.

Developing Practice Plans

Coaches rarely believe they have enough time to practice everything they want to cover. Therefore, you must set and agree on priorities concerning how the practices will be conducted and the actual amount of time to allocate for each part of the practice. Although your practice structure will vary slightly depending on where you are in your season, each practice plan should include the following sections:

- Purpose
- Equipment
- Plan

The purpose of a practice focuses on what you want to teach your players; it outlines the main theme for the practice and should be drawn from your season plan. Equipment sections note what you need to have on hand for each practice. Plan sections are the core of what you will do during practice. Plan sections consist of the following basic elements:

Warm-Up (5 to 10 minutes)

During the warm-up, the entire team is arranged in predetermined rows and positions. This type of setup lets you see easily who is absent from practice. Use brisk running to raise the core temperature of each player during this period.

Cool-Down (5 to 10 minutes)

Use the cool-down to bring the team together and run either offensive plays down the field or team pursuit or interception defenses against the air as a group. This is a conditioning period using a football activity, followed by a short stretching period in groups.

The remaining elements of the plan section vary both in structure and in content depending on where you are in the season. However, elements that may be used in multiple practices are as follows:

Introduction (5 minutes)

This period can be used to introduce a new offensive play or a new defense depending on the focus of the day. It should be short and to the point.

Individual Period (15 minutes)

During this period, teach individual techniques to the various groups. The size of your coaching staff will determine the number of groups. Keep the drills short, teach one technique in each drill, and allow each player the maximum number of repetitions.

Group Period (20 minutes)

Use this time for groups to play against one another. The drills that you use will vary from one practice to the other. The following are examples:

- Passing drills with the receivers running routes against defensive backs
- Pass protection drills with the offensive line working against the defensive line
- Half-team assignments against half defenses
- Techniques in the one-on-one drills and assignments in the half-line drills

Special Teams Period (10 minutes)

Focus on one or more of the special teams segments that you need for the game. Try to work on corresponding parts of the kicking game. For example, work on the kickoff team and kickoff return team at the same time.

Team Period (20 minutes)

Work the entire offense versus the entire defense at this time. During the offensive segment, the defense acts as the opponent by running the opponent's defense or offensive plays and vice versa during the defensive segment. The major focus should be on timing, assignments, and working as a unit.

If you have players who play both offense and defense, you may need to organize your practice schedule so that one day is an offensive day and the next is a defensive day. Players playing both offense and defense can then focus on one phase of their preparation on each day. Inform players what the emphasis will be before the warm-up period at the start of practice.

Practice Types

As was discussed earlier in this chapter, you will vary your practices based on where you are in your season. The main parts of the season are the preseason and the regular season.

Preseason Practices

League rules will require that a certain number of practices at the beginning of the season be conducted without pads. Use the first two of these practices to introduce individual techniques, work on conditioning, and establish practice organization. These two practice sessions should be devoted to giving every player a chance to try out for any position and to find the players that have the best natural skills required to play specific positions on the team. For an example of this type of practice refer to "Sample Plan for the First Two Preseason Practices."

Sample Plan for the First Two Preseason Practices

The first two practice sessions of the preseason should be devoted to giving every player a chance to try out for any position and to find the players on the team that have the best natural skills (throwing, catching, running fast, punting, and kicking) required to play specific positions on the team. These practices should be run without pads.

Purpose
To give every player a chance to try out for any position and to find the players on the team who have the best natural skills required to play specific positions.

Equipment
Players should wear mouth guards, helmets, T-shirts, shorts or football pants, socks, and football shoes and should bring water. Coaches should provide five or more footballs, a whistle, clipboard, forms for recording notes on players, kickoff tee, field goal tee, water, and a basic first aid kit with a cell phone.

Warm-Up (10 minutes)
Each player lines up for the start of practice. The order of the player lineup can be identified at the first early preseason practice. The lineup can be determined by position or a combination of positions in one line. Explain that this is the order in which players should line up at the start of each practice and for pregame warm-ups. Keep a chart so that you can easily look out and see who is missing. Once the players are lined up, conduct a short stretching period, a set of 10 push-ups, a set of 10 sit-ups, and then run strides across the field to raise players' core temperature for practice.

Open Throwing Drill (15 to 20 minutes)

All players who want to try out for quarterback should have the chance. With very young players you could substitute a softball for a football. Have players throw to their right and to their left for accuracy to players running slant routes and then hook routes, and then have them throw deep on up routes. Have two quarterbacks throw at a time and keep the lines moving. Evaluate natural arm strength and accuracy without coaching. Always keep a written record.

Open Punting Drill (15 to 20 minutes)

Any player who wants to punt should be given the opportunity. Allow each player to take five punts. Evaluate natural leg strength and accuracy without coaching. Always keep a written record. Arrange the other players in two lines to try to catch punts.

Open Receiving Drill (15 to 20 minutes)

All players who want to be a wide receiver should be given the opportunity. The other players can fill in at the tight end positions. Explain and demonstrate the three pass routes that will be run. Spread four lines across the field and have two coaches throwing the ball. The two lines closest to the quarterback run tight end routes and the two wide lines run wide receiver routes. Start with a slant and look-in route combination, an all-hook combination, and then an up route by the wide receivers and a post route by the tight ends. Evaluate the natural ability of each player without coaching. Always keep a written record.

Open Kickoff Drill (15 to 20 minutes)

Any player who wants to kick off should be given the opportunity. Allow each kicker to take five kicks. Evaluate natural leg strength and kicking skill without coaching. Always keep a written record. Arrange other players in two lines to try to catch kicks.

Interception Drill (15 to 20 minutes)

Divide the team into four groups. Spread the team into four lines across the field, 10 yards down the field facing the coach (one coach is on each side of the field). The coach points the ball at the first player in line. The player runs in place and the coach throws the ball with the player making the interception and running the ball back to the coach. Evaluate the natural ability of each player from a defensive position without coaching. Always keep a written record.

Cool-Down (10 minutes)

Finish the practice and bring the team together in their original positions. Lead cool-down stretches and explain the next practice session. After the practice, evaluate the players based on your records and watching them perform and begin to determine where players will be best suited to play.

The practices that follow these first two practice sessions can be used to condition your team; to introduce the players to your practice schedule, offense, defense, and special teams; and to prepare players to practice in pads later in the season. Practices without pads at the start of the year are a good time to get players lined up properly on offense, defense, and special teams and to focus on teaching individual techniques against the air. Move the players into different positions to give them experience playing different positions and to help you evaluate where a player should line up. A template, "Preseason Practices (No Pads)," can be found in appendix A on page 175. You can use this template to guide you when designing practices for this part of your season.

After your required practices without pads you will begin your preseason practices with the players in full uniform. Use the practices with pads at the start of the year to introduce your base offense, defense, and special teams. Focus on teaching the individual skills needed to play each position, then begin bringing the players together so that they can start to function as an 11-player unit and get used to contact. This practice can be broken into small groups; the number depends on the size of your staff. A template, "Preseason Practices (Pads)," can be found in appendix A on page 174. You can use this template to guide you when designing practices for this part of your season.

Preseason sessions also include practices with pads before a scrimmage. These practices prepare the team for the scrimmage by reviewing how players will line up for stretching, where they will go, and what they will do to warm up. Review all the substitutions for offense, defense, and special teams during this practice. Eliminate all but half-speed contact from this practice. Do not run the players excessively; keep their legs and minds fresh. A template, "Preseason Practice Before First Scrimmage (Pads)," can be found in appendix A on page 176. You can use this template to guide you when designing this type of practice.

Regular Season Practices

You will conduct your regular season practices with pads according to your practice plan once the regular season is underway. If you have a limited staff or if several players play both offense and defense, you may want to designate one practice as an offensive day and the next practice as a defensive day. This method is especially well suited to introducing the walk-through, the individual period, and the emphasis during the group and team segments of your practice. A template, "Regular Season Practices (Pads)," can be found in appendix A on page 177. You can use this template to guide you when designing practices during this part of your season.

Regular season practices with pads before game day prepare the team for the game by reviewing how they will line up for stretching, where they will go, and what they will do for a warm-up. Review all the substitutions for offense, defense, and special teams during this practice. Eliminate all but half-speed contact from this practice. Do not run the players excessively during a practice right before a game. Keep their legs rested and their minds fresh. A template, "Regular Season Practices Before Game Day (Pads)," can be found in appendix A on page 178. You can use this template to guide you when designing this type of practices.

Fun Learning Environment

Regardless of where you are in your season, it is important that you create an environment that welcomes learning and promotes teamwork. Following are seven tips that will help you and your staff get the most out of your practices:

1. Stick to the practice times agreed upon as a staff.
2. Start and end each practice as a team.
3. Keep the practice routine as consistent as possible so that the players can feel comfortable.
4. Be organized in your approach by moving quickly from one drill to another and from one period to another.
5. Tell your players what the practice will include before the practice starts.
6. Allow the players to take water breaks whenever possible.
7. Focus on providing positive feedback.

You may also want to consider using games to make practices more fun. In appendix C, beginning on page 182, you will find 15 gamelike drills. During your season, it may be fun to use the games toward the end of the week to add variety to your practices. Modify games so that there is no contact when you are holding practices without pads.

Appendix A

Related Checklists and Forms

This appendix contains checklists and forms that will be useful in your football program. All checklists and forms mentioned in the text can be found here. You may reproduce and use these forms as needed for your football program.

Facilities and Equipment Checklist

Field Surface

❑ Sprinkler heads and openings are at grass level.

❑ The field is free of toxic substances (lime, fertilizer, and so on).

❑ The playing surface is free of debris.

❑ No rocks or cement slabs are on the field.

❑ The field is free of protruding pipes, wires, and lines.

❑ The field is not too wet.

❑ The field is not too dry.

❑ The field lines are well marked.

Outside Playing Area

❑ The edge of the playing field is at least six feet from trees, walls, fences, and cars.

❑ Nearby buildings are protected by fences or walls from possible damage during play.

❑ Storage sheds and facilities are locked.

❑ The playground area, including ground surface and equipment, is safe and in good condition.

❑ The fences or walls lining the area are in good repair.

❑ Sidewalks are without cracks, separations, or raised concrete.

Equipment

❑ Goals are held together securely.

❑ Players' equipment has been checked as specified in the "Player Equipment Checklist."

From *Coaching Youth Football, Fourth Edition,* by ASEP, 2005, Champaign, IL: Human Kinetics.

Informed Consent Form

I hereby give my permission for _____ to participate in _____ during the athletic season beginning on _____. Further, I authorize the school to provide emergency treatment of any injury or illness my child may experience if qualified medical personnel consider treatment necessary and perform the treatment. This authorization is granted only if I cannot be reached and reasonable effort has been made to do so.

Parent or guardian: _____

Address: _____ **Phone:** (   )_____

Cell phone: (   )_____ **Beeper number:** (   )_____

Other person to contact in case of emergency: _____

Relationship to person: _____ **Phone:** (   )_____

Family physician: _____ **Phone:** (   )_____

Medical conditions (e.g., allergies, chronic illness): _____
_____
_____
_____

My child and I are aware that participating in _____ is a potentially hazardous activity. We assume all risks associated with participation in this sport, including but not limited to falls, contact with other participants, and the effects of the weather, traffic, and other reasonable-risk conditions associated with the sport. All such risks to my child are known and appreciated by my child and me.

We understand this informed consent form and agree to its conditions.

Child's signature: _____ **Date:** _____

Parent's or guardian's signature: _____ **Date:** _____

Reprinted, by permission, from ASEP, 1993, *Rookie coaches football guide* (Champaign, IL: Human Kinetics), 28.

Player Equipment Checklist

It is important to keep your player equipment safe. Use this checklist to frequently check the equipment of your players.

☐ **Shoulder pads** Body padding should not extend beyond the tip of the shoulder; neck area should fit snugly when arms are extended overhead.

☐ **Helmet** Helmet must fit snugly around the head and in the jaw section; head should be in contact with crown suspension when the front edge is approximately one inch above the eyebrow.

☐ **Clothing** Jersey should fit close to the body and should always be tucked into the pants to hold shoulder pads in place; pants should hug the body to keep thigh and knee guards in place.

☐ **Mouth guard** Mouth guard should fit properly.

☐ **Girdle pads** Hip pads must cover the point of the hip and give proper lower-spine protection.

☐ **Thigh and knee pads** Thigh and knee pads must be the proper size and inserted properly in the lining of the player's pants.

☐ **Shoes** Cleats should be inspected regularly to ensure even wear and stability; proper width is very important; upper should never "overrun" outsole.

From *Coaching Youth Football, Fourth Edition,* by ASEP, 2005, Champaign, IL: Human Kinetics.

Injury Report Form

Date: _____ Time: _____a.m. p.m.

Athlete's name: _____

Type of injury: _____

Anatomical area involved: _____

Cause of injury: _____

Extent of injury: _____

Person administering first aid (name): _____

First aid administered: _____

Other treatment administered: _____

Referral action: _____

Person administering first aid (signature): _____

Date: _____

Emergency Information Card

Athlete's name: _____ Sport: _____

Age: _____

S.S. #: _____

Address: _____

Phone: _____

Provide information for parent or guardian and one additional contact in case of emergency.

Parent's or guardian's name: _____

Address: _____

Phone: _____

Other phone: _____

Additional contact's name: _____

Relationship to athlete: _____

Address: _____

Phone: _____

Other phone: _____

Insurance Information

Name of insurance company: _____

Policy name and number: _____

Medical Information

Physician's name: _____

Phone: _____

Is your child allergic to any drugs?   *Yes   No*

If so, what? _____

Does your child have any other allergies (e.g., bee stings, dust)? _____

Does your child have any of the following?   *asthma   diabetes   epilepsy*

Is your child currently taking medication? *Yes   No*

If so, what? _____

Does your child wear contact lenses?   *Yes   No*

Is there additional information we should know about your child's health or physical condition?   *Yes   No*

If yes, please explain: _____

Parent's or guardian's signature: _____ Date: _____

From *Coaching Youth Football, Fourth Edition,* by ASEP, 2005, Champaign, IL: Human Kinetics.

Emergency Response Card

Be prepared to give the following information to an EMS dispatcher. Note: Do not hang up first. Let the EMS dispatcher hang up first.

Caller's name: _____

Telephone number from which the call is being made: _____

Reason for call: _____

How many people are injured: _____

Condition of victim(s): _____

First aid being given: _____

Location: _____

Address: _____

City: _____

Directions (e.g., cross streets, landmarks, entrance access, etc.):

Preseason Practices (Pads)

Purpose

Equipment

Warm-Up *(10 minutes)*

Introduction of New Plays *(10 minutes)*

Individual Period *(20 minutes)*

Special Teams Period *(10 minutes)*

Group Period *(15 minutes)*

Offensive Team Period *(20 minutes)*

Defensive Team Period *(20 minutes)*

Conditioning *(10 minutes)*

Cool-Down *(5 minutes)*

From *Coaching Youth Football, Fourth Edition,* by ASEP, 2005, Champaign, IL: Human Kinetics.

Preseason Practices (No Pads)

Purpose

Equipment

Warm-Up *(5-10 minutes)*

Offensive Period 1 *(20 minutes)*

Defensive Period 1 *(10 minutes)*

Special Teams Period *(20 minutes)*

Offensive Period 2 *(20 minutes)*

Defensive Period 2 *(20 minutes)*

Cool-Down *(5-10 minutes)*

From *Coaching Youth Football, Fourth Edition,* by ASEP, 2005, Champaign, IL: Human Kinetics.

Preseason Practice Before First Scrimmage (Pads)

Purpose

Equipment

Warm-Up *(5-10 minutes)*

Individual Period *(15 minutes)*
Use this time to cover the individual warm-up used at scrimmage.

Sideline Substitution Review *(20 minutes)*
Use this time to practice all substitutions for offense, defense, and special teams by having players run on and off the field.

Kicking Review *(20 minutes)*
Use this time to review all phases of the kicking game.

Offensive Review *(20 minutes)*
Use this time to review the first 10 plays that the offense will run.

Defensive Review *(20 minutes)*
Use this time to review base fronts and pass coverages for defense.

Cool-Down *(5-10 minutes)*
Use this time to review time structure and location of scrimmage. Be positive and emphasize that the scrimmage is a learning situation.

From *Coaching Youth Football, Fourth Edition,* by ASEP, 2005, Champaign, IL: Human Kinetics.

Regular Season Practices (Pads)

Purpose

Equipment

Warm-Up *(5-10 minutes)*

Introduction of New Plays *(5 minutes)*

Individual Period *(15 minutes)*

Special Teams Period *(10 minutes)*

Group Period *(20 minutes)*

Offensive Period *(20 minutes)*

Defensive Period *(20 minutes)*

Cool-Down and Conditioning *(5-10 minutes)*

From *Coaching Youth Football, Fourth Edition,* by ASEP, 2005, Champaign, IL: Human Kinetics.

Regular Season Practices Before Game Day (Pads)

Purpose

Equipment

Warm-Up *(10 minutes)*

Individual Period *(10 minutes)*

Sideline Substitution Review *(10 minutes)*

Kicking Review *(20 minutes)*

Offensive Review *(20 minutes)*

Defensive Review *(15 minutes)*

Cool-Down *(5 minutes)*

From *Coaching Youth Football, Fourth Edition,* by ASEP, 2005, Champaign, IL: Human Kinetics.

Appendix B

Football Terms

audible—a vocal signal at the line of scrimmage to change the play previously called in the huddle.

backfield—players who are 1 yard or more behind the scrimmage line when the ball is snapped, including quarterback, running backs, and wing back.

blitz—a play in which the defense commits extra players, in addition to linemen, to rush the passer.

chains—ten-yard length of chain used to measure the distance required for a first down.

cross block—a block in which two linemen block defenders who are diagonally opposite the blockers' own starting positions; one of the blockers, usually the outside blocker, goes in front.

defensive formation—an alignment of defensive linemen, linebackers, and defensive backs positioned to stop a particular offense.

downs—a series of four consecutive charged scrimmages allotted to the offensive team; to retain possession, the offense must advance the ball 10 yards to a yard line called the necessary line during these scrimmages.

eligible receiver—any offensive player who is legally in the backfield or any player on either end of the line of scrimmage.

end zone—the area bounded by the goal line, end line, and sidelines.

fair catch—an unhindered catch by a member of the receiving team of any kick that has crossed the kicking team's line of scrimmage or free-kick line, provided that the proper signal (one hand and arm extended above the head and moving from side to side) has been given by the receiver.

field goal—a placekick or dropkick from scrimmage that goes over the crossbar and through the uprights of the goal without touching the ground first. Three points are awarded for a field goal.

first down—the first of four allotted downs the offensive team receives, occurring when the offensive team gains 10 or more yards within its allotted four downs.

forward pass—a pass that strikes anything beyond the spot from which it was thrown; a pass in the direction of the opponent's goal.

fumble—losing possession of the football by means other than by passing or kicking it.

goal line defense—defensive alignment used near the defensive team's own goal line that features defensive players driving for penetration through the gaps and has all defensive players close to the line of scrimmage in an attempt to stop the offensive team from scoring a touchdown by running or passing the ball across the goal line.

goal post—a structure located on each end line; attempts at field goals and extra points must pass over the crossbar and through the goal posts to be successful.

handoff—the action of handing (not passing or throwing laterally) the ball from one player to another. The quarterback usually executes a handoff to a running back, but a running back might also execute a handoff to the receiver on a reverse.

hash mark—the line running the length of the field bisecting the yard lines. The ball is not placed outside the hash marks when a play is to begin.

I-formation—the offensive formation in which a fullback and tailback are positioned in a line directly behind the quarterback; the center, quarterback, fullback, and tailback form the letter I.

illegal use of hands—with possession of the ball established by either team, a player's using the hands to grasp and impede an opponent who is not a ball carrier.

ineligible receiver—a player on the line of scrimmage, with at least one other player on either side of him, who cannot legally catch a pass or, on a pass play, be downfield before a pass is thrown.

interception—the action of gaining possession of the ball when a defender catches a pass thrown by the offense.

kickoff—a free kick initiating each half of a game; it also follows the scoring of a field goal and a touchdown and extra point attempt. The ball is either placed on the kicking team's 40-yard line on a kicking tee or held by a player on the kicking team. All players on the kicking team must remain behind their 40-yard line until the ball is kicked. Once the ball travels 10 yards downfield, either team can establish possession.

kickoff return—the action of a team receiving a kickoff to establish possession of the ball and to attempt to advance the ball upfield.

late hit—an infraction occurring when a player hits an opponent after the play is over by rule.

lateral pass—a pass in which the ball is tossed or thrown backward. (If it is dropped, it is considered a fumble.)

line of scrimmage—an imaginary line running perpendicular to the sidelines. The offensive and defensive lines of scrimmage are located on either end of the neutral zone and mark the ball's position at the start of each down.

man-to-man coverage—defensive pass coverage in which defenders are assigned specific receivers to cover; they cover those receivers no matter where they run their routes and only leave their man when he blocks, the ball is thrown, or the ball carrier crosses the line of scrimmage.

neutral zone—the area located within the width of the football field.

offensive formation—the offensive team's lineup, or the offensive players' locations, before the snap of the ball.

onside kick—a play in which a kickoff is deliberately kicked short so that the team kicking off has a chance to gain possession of the ball.

option—an offensive play designed to give the ball carrier, usually the quarterback, the opportunity to carry the ball up the field, hand the ball off, or pass it to a teammate.

passing route—the path a receiver takes in an attempt to get open to receive a pass (or to serve as a decoy).

pass rush—a defender's attempt to tackle or hurry a member of the offensive team attempting to pass the football.

placekick—an action in which the ball is kicked from a tee or from the hold of a member of the kicking team; used for field goals and kickoffs.

play action pass—a play in which a fake handoff precedes a pass attempt; this pass is designed to pull in the linebackers and defensive backs and to slow the pass rush (by making the defense think the play is a run).

possession—having control of the ball.

punt—kicking the ball after dropping it and before it reaches the ground. Offensive teams who have failed to cover 10 yards in their first three attempts often punt on the fourth down.

punt coverage—the action of the players of the punting team running downfield when the ball is punted in an attempt to tackle the opponent who has fielded the punted ball if it has not been called for a fair catch.

punt return—the action of the player who has received a punted ball in trying to advance it.

quarterback sneak—a play in which a quarterback runs or dives over the line of scrimmage.

roughing the passer—an infraction that occurs when a defensive player hits the quarterback after the ball has been released. The official must decide whether the defensive player had time to stop after the ball's release.

sack—the action of a defender tackling the quarterback on an attempted pass play behind the line of scrimmage.

shotgun—an offensive formation in which the quarterback is lined up in the backfield 4 to 6 yards behind the center.

snap—the quick exchange of the football from the center to the quarterback to put the ball into play.

T-formation—an offensive formation in which the fullback is positioned 2 to 4 yards behind a quarterback who is positioned immediately behind the center. One halfback is on either side of the fullback, and the fullback and the two halfbacks are in a line parallel to the line of scrimmage.

time-out—an event in which the clock is stopped at the request of a player from either team. In general, each team is allowed three requests during each half of a game.

touchback—a situation in which the ball is kicked through the end zone or downed in the receiving team's end zone. Play restarts on the receiving team's 20-yard line.

trap block—a technique in which offensive linemen pull laterally from their original position on the offensive side of the line of scrimmage and block an unsuspecting defender elsewhere down the line or in the defensive backfield.

two-point conversion—A play in which the offense successfully runs or passes the ball into the end zone from the 3-yard line following a touchdown.

wishbone—an offensive formation in which the quarterback is under center (direct snap), a fullback is directly behind the quarterback, and two halfbacks are behind and to the sides of the fullback.

zone coverage—defensive pass coverage in which defenders are assigned specific areas to cover and focus on the quarterback and react to the area of the field where the ball is thrown.

Appendix C

15 Gamelike Drills

The 15 gamelike drills found here are for use in your football program. As a youth football coach, you will want to use gamelike drills during practices to help keep motivation and interest high and to keep the sport fun.

Drive-Through

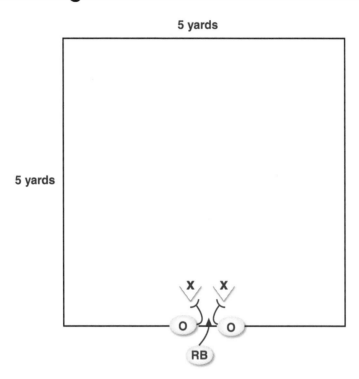

5 yards

5 yards

Goal

To use drive blocking to open holes for the ball carrier

Description

Play 3v2 or 4v3 in a 5-square-yard area. The offense and defense start opposite each other on one of the boundary lines. The game begins with the offensive line's first move. The offense gets one point every time it keeps the defense from tackling the running back—or ball carrier. The defense gets one point each time it tackles the ball carrier. Each team gets three consecutive plays. Because teams score based on whether or not the ball carrier gets tackled rather than how many yards are gained, each play can begin where the other play ended. However, if players get close to the boundaries, flip the teams around and have the offense move down the field in the opposite direction. Rotate players to maintain the same number of blockers and defenders.

Variations

- To make the game easier, widen the playing area or have the defense play at half or three-quarters speed.
- To make the game more difficult, narrow the playing area or have the defense play at full speed.

The Escort

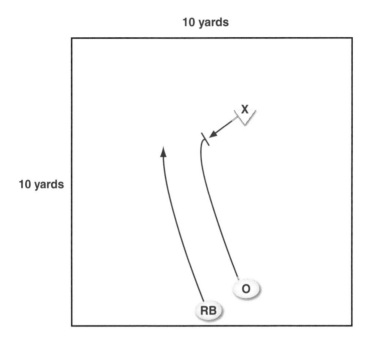

Goal

To gain yardage by blocking downfield for the ball carrier

Description

Play 2v1 or 3v2 in a 10-square-yard area. Blockers and defenders start at least 5 yards apart anywhere inside the playing area. The game begins with the blocker's first move. The offense gets one point every time it keeps the defense from tackling the running back—or ball carrier. The defense gets one point each time it tackles the ball carrier. Switch offense and defense after three plays, rotating players to maintain the same number of players on offense and defense.

Variations

- To make the game easier, widen the playing area or play 3v1 or 4v2.
- To make the game more difficult, narrow the playing area or play 2v2 or 3v3.

Protecting the QB

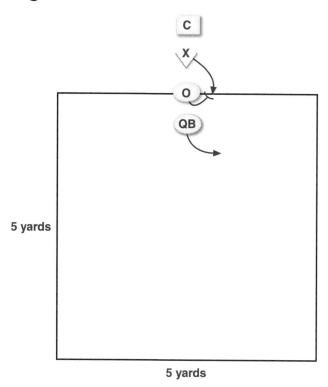

5 yards

5 yards

Goal

To use pass protection blocking to keep defensive players from getting to the quarterback

Description

Play 2v1 or 3v2 in a 5-square-yard area using a quarterback and one or two offensive line players and one or two defensive line players. The offense and defense start opposite each other on one of the boundary lines. The coach stands behind the defense and signals the start count to the offense. On the count, the blocker or blockers move into pass protection blocking as the quarterback drops back to pass. The blockers must keep the defense from getting to the quarterback for at least 5 seconds. The offense gets one point for keeping the defense away from the quarterback. The defense gets one point for touching the quarterback.

Variations

- To make the game easier, give the defense only 3 seconds to touch the quarterback or play 3v1 or 4v2.
- To make the game more difficult, give the defense 7 seconds to touch the quarterback or play 2v2 or 3v3.

Screen Door

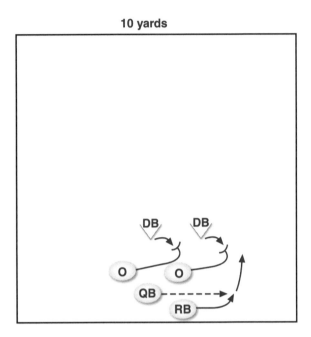

10 yards

Goal

To use screen blocking to keep defenders from the ball carrier

Description

Play 4v2 in a 10-yard-wide playing area. A quarterback, running back, and two blockers will play offense; two defensive backs will play defense. The quarterback begins with the ball. On the quarterback's signal, the play begins and the running back receives a swing pass in the flat. The running back then follows his blockers and tries to elude the defenders. The offense gets one point each time the running back is able to elude the defenders by using the blockers. The defense scores one point each time it tackles the running back. Rotate players every three plays.

Variations

- To make the game easier, widen the playing area or play 4v1 or 5v2.
- To make the game more difficult, narrow the playing area or play 4v3.

Follow the Leader

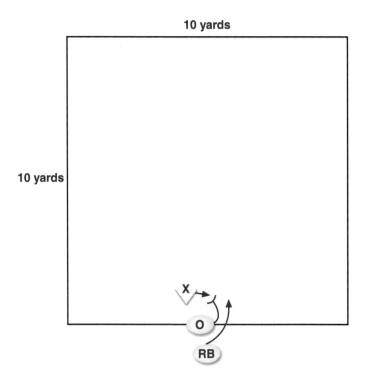

10 yards

10 yards

Goal

To use blockers as a shield between the ball carrier and defenders

Description

Play 2v1 in a 10-square-yard area. Blockers line up on one of the boundary lines and use a hand behind the back to signal which way the ball carrier should go and on what count. The running back stands behind the blockers and outside the playing area holding the ball. The blocker's first move initiates the play. The offense gets one point each time it gains 10 yards in one play. The defense gets one point each time it stops the offense from gaining 10 yards. Rotate players after a running back has run three straight turns with the ball.

Variations

- To make the game easier, widen the playing area.
- To make the game more difficult, narrow the playing area or play 3v2 or 4v3.

Catching On

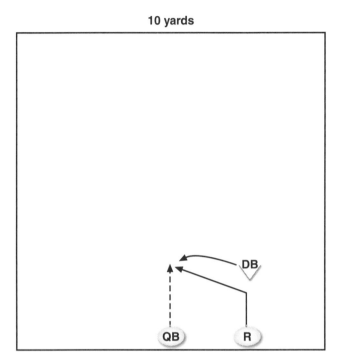

10 yards

Goal

To catch the ball

Description

Play 2v1 or 3v2 in an area 10 yards wide. You can vary the length of the playing area, but it should be at least 10 yards long, and probably should not exceed 20 yards. The quarterback tells the receiver or receivers what route to run and the count to start on. Play begins on the count specified by the quarterback. The offense gets one point each time it completes a pass, and the defense, which includes a defensive back, gets one point each time it prevents a receiver from catching the ball. Rotate offensive players after three consecutive plays.

Variations

- To make the game easier, move receivers closer to the quarterback or play 3v1 or 4v2.
- To make the game more difficult, move the receiver farther away from the quarterback, play 2v2 or 3v3, or have the defense play at full speed.

Air Ball

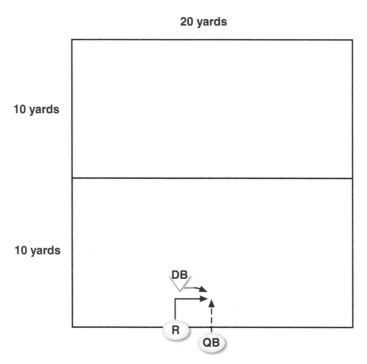

20 yards

10 yards

10 yards

Goal

To pass the ball down the field and score

Description

Play 2v1 or 3v2 in a 20-square-yard area with goal lines at each length of the area and a 10-yard line across the middle of the area. The offense begins on the goal line. The quarterback tells the receiver or receivers what route to run. The play begins on the quarterback's count. Once the play begins, the quarterback drops back to make the pass, as shown in the figure. The offense gets three plays to advance the ball 20 yards to the opposite goal line and gets one point for passing the 10-yard line in the middle of the area and an additional point for passing the 20-yard goal line. The defense gets one point if the offense doesn't get past the 20-yard goal line and two points if it doesn't get past the 10-yard line in the middle of the area. After a team advances past the 20-yard goal line or after three plays, switch offense and defense, rotating players to maintain the offensive advantage.

Variations

- To make the game easier, widen the playing area to 30 yards or play 4v2 or 5v3.
- To make the game more difficult, play 2v2 or 3v3 or make the field 15 yards wide or 30 yards deep or both.

Hit the Hole

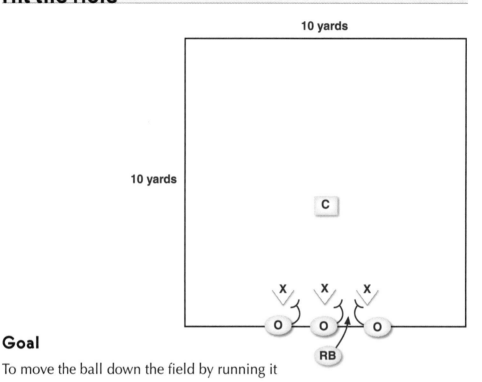

10 yards

10 yards

Goal

To move the ball down the field by running it

Description

Play 4v3 in a 10-square-yard area with goal lines at each end of the playing area. Three defensive players are lined up inside the playing area 2 to 3 feet off the goal line. Three offensive players are lined up on the goal line, and a running back, with the ball, is lined up behind them and outside the playing area. The coach stands behind the defensive players also inside the playing area and signals to the offense where the ball is to be run by pointing to a specific spot in the playing area without letting the defense see where he is pointing.

On the running back's signal, play begins. The running back runs through the area where the coach pointed and attempts to gain as many yards as possible. The offense has three chances to score. The next play begins where the running back was tackled. If the offense can score within three plays, it gets a point. If the offense can't score, the defense gets a point. Switch offense and defense after the offense scores or after it runs three plays, rotating players to maintain the 4v3 offensive advantage.

Variations

- To make the game easier, widen the playing area to 15 or 20 yards or play 4v2.
- To make the game more difficult, lengthen the playing area to 15 or 20 yards or play 4v4.

Heads Up

Goal

To execute the proper head-on tackling form in tackling the ball carrier

Description

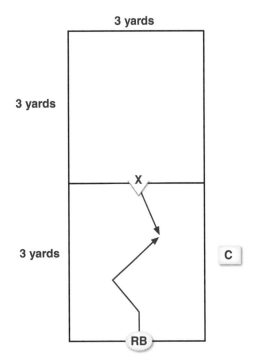

3 yards

3 yards

3 yards

Play 1v1 in an area 3 yards wide by 6 yards long with a line of scrimmage across the middle of the playing area. A running back—or ball carrier—and a defender line up facing each other with the defender on the line of scrimmage and the running back on a boundary line at one end of the playing area. The running back's goal is to get past the defender and get to the other end of the playing area. In other words, gain 3 yards beyond the line of scrimmage. The defender's goal is to tackle the ball carrier using proper form before the ball carrier gains these 3 yards.

The play begins on the coach's command. Defenders get one point for keeping their heads up, one point for wrapping their arms around the ball carrier, one point for taking the ball carrier down, and two points for stopping the runner from gaining the 3 yards beyond the line of scrimmage. The running back gets three points for gaining 3 or more yards. The running back should run three times and then switch positions with the defender.

Note: Before the players begin, instruct all players to keep their heads up as they attempt to tackle and to slide their heads to the outside just before making contact.

Variations

- To make the game easier, the running back must gain 5 yards before awarding the three points or move the players closer together.
- To make the game more difficult, widen the playing area, move the players farther apart, or award the running back three points for gaining yardage.
- The game can be adapted for angle and open-field tackling by making the playing area larger and adjusting players' positioning.

No-Passing Zone

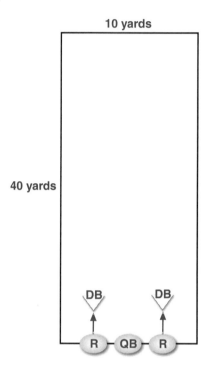

Goal

To intercept the pass or prevent it from being completed

Description

Play 3v2 or 4v3 in an area 10 yards wide by 40 yards long with goal lines at each end of the area. Receivers are positioned on a goal line at one end of the area and defensive backs are positioned inside the playing area to start. The quarterback is also positioned on the goal line with the ball and signals the play to start. Receivers run straight down the field and run whatever pattern they want. The defensive backs can play either man-to-man or zone defense and must backpedal and break to the ball when it is thrown. The defense gets two points for intercepting a pass and one point for preventing a receiver from catching the ball or causing a receiver to drop the ball. If an offensive player catches the ball, the defenders must tackle the ball carrier. After three plays, switch defense and offense, maintaining the same number of players on each side. If the offense is able to gain 40 yards (or more if they lost yardage and later picked it up), crossing the opposite goal line within the three plays, any points gained by the defense are wiped out.

Variations

- To make the game easier, lengthen the playing area or play 3v3 or 3v4.
- To make the game more difficult, shorten the playing area.

Airtight D

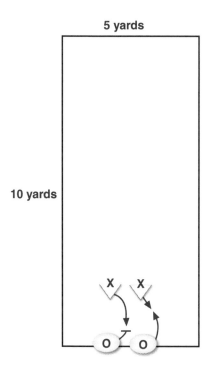

Goal

To stop the play at or behind the line of scrimmage

Description

Play 2v2 or 3v3 in an area 5 yards wide by 10 yards long with goal lines at each end of the area. The offensive players are positioned on a goal line at one end of the area, and defensive players are positioned inside the playing area. Play starts on the offensive movement, which is initiated by a signal from the coach. The defense gets one point each time it prevents the offense from gaining yardage. The offense is allowed three downs to gain 10 yards and gets three points each time it does so. Rotate defense and offense when the offense gains 10 yards or when it has completed the three downs.

Variations

- To make the game easier, lengthen the playing area to 20 yards or play 2v3 or 3v4.
- To make the game more difficult, widen the playing area to 10 yards or play 3v2 or 4v3.

Large and In Charge

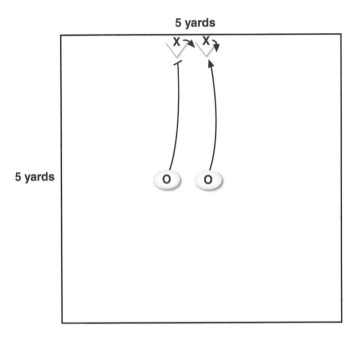

Goal

To keep the offense from gaining the last 3 yards

Description

Play 2v2 or 3v3 in an area 5 yards wide by 5 yards long with goal lines on each end. The offense positions approximately 3 yards from its goal. The defense positions along the goal line. The defense gets two points each time it prevents the offense from scoring. The offense gets two points when it scores. Rotate defense and offense after four plays.

Variations

- To make the game easier on the defense, give the offense just one down to score.
- To make the game more difficult on the defense, give the offense three downs to score.

Field Position

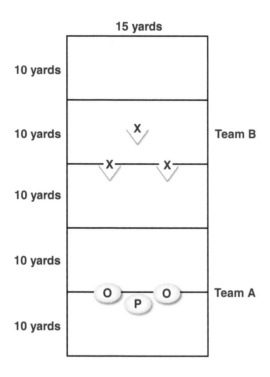

Goal

To gain better field position than the other team through returning punts and defending against returned punts

Description

Play 3v3 in an area 15 yards wide by 50 yards deep. Team A lines up on the 10-yard line and punts to team B. Team B returns the punt as far as possible. Team B then lines up where they were tackled and punts the ball back to team A, which returns the ball as far as it can. Play continues until each team has made three punts. The team with the best field position wins the game.

Variations

- To make the game easier for offense and more difficult for defense, widen the playing area or put an additional player on the receiving team.
- To make the game more difficult for offense and easier for defense, narrow the playing area or put an additional player on the punting team.

Trifecta

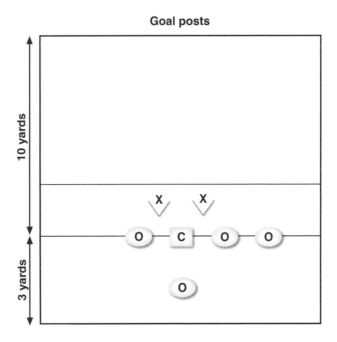

Goal

To kick the ball from a placekicking tee through the goalpost uprights

Description

Play 5v2 or 7v4 with the ball placed 13 yards from the goalposts. Defensive and offensive players line up on the 13-yard line. Play starts when the center hikes the ball to the placekick holder, who places the ball on the tee. The defensive players cannot hit the center, but they can attempt to block the kick. The kicking team gets three points for each successful kick. Each team gets three consecutive kicks.

Variations

- To make the game easier, shorten the length of the kick or start play with the placekick holder moving to place the ball on the tee.
- To make the game more difficult, lengthen the kick, add another defensive player, or move the ball to the left or right rather than kicking from the center.

Kicking Into Gear

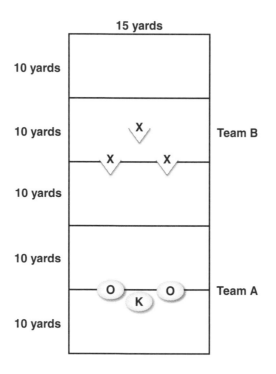

Goal

To provide kickers an opportunity to kick from the tee in a gamelike situation

Description

Play 3v3 in an area 15 yards wide by 50 yards deep. Team A (who will kick first, using a tee) lines up on the 10-yard line and kicks off to team B, who returns the kickoff as far as possible. Team B then lines up where they were tackled and kicks off back to team A, which returns the ball as far as it can. Play continues until each team has kicked off three times. The team with the best field position wins the game.

Variations

- To make the game easier for offense and more difficult for defense, widen the playing area or add a player to the receiving team.
- To make the game more difficult for offense and easier for defense, narrow the playing area or add a player to the kicking team.

About the Author

Coaching Youth Football was written by the American Sport Education Program (ASEP) in conjunction with USA Football and former NFL coach and youth football advocate Tom Bass. The NFL and NFL Players Association launched USA Football through a grant from the NFL Youth Football Fund. This independent nonprofit organization's purpose is to galvanize, support, promote, and expand the sport at all levels of amateur football. ASEP is a division of Human Kinetics, based in Champaign, Illinois, and has been developing and delivering coaches education courses since 1981. As the nation's number one coaching education program, ASEP works with national, state, and local youth sport organizations to develop educational programs for coaches, officials, administrators, and parents. These programs incorporate ASEP's philosophy of "Athletes first...Winning second."

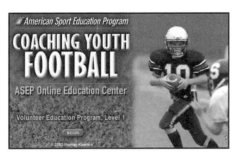